Submarine!

With a shattering explosion, an American torpedo makes a direct hit on a Japanese aircraft carrier. The sub crew hastily prepares for the getaway.

Submarine!

THE STORY OF UNDERSEA FIGHTERS

BY KENDALL BANNING

ILLUSTRATED BY CHARLES ROSNER

COACHWHIP PUBLICATIONS
GREENVILLE, OHIO

Acknowledgments

The acknowledgments of the author are gratefully extended to the Navy Department in Washington; to Captain Elwin F. Cutts, Commandant of the Naval Base at New London, Conn.; to Commander Carroll T. Bonney, Executive Officer at the Naval Base; to Commander Karl G. Hensel, Commandant of the Submarine School, and to Mrs. Hensel; and to Lieutenant D. H. Byerly, Public Relations Officer, for their co-operation in the compiling and checking of the information in this book.

Bauer's Submarine

Submarine!, by Kendall Banning (1879-1944)
© 2024 Coachwhip Publications edition

First published 1942 / Illustrated by Charles Rosner (1894-1975)
CoachwhipBooks.com

ISBN 1-61646-579-4
ISBN-13 978-1-61646-579-7

Contents

The *American Turtle* Surfaces

CHAPTER I

The Submarine Is Born

THE submarine is an American invention. It is as much a "Yankee notion" as the telephone and telegraph, the cotton gin, the steamship, the electric light, the airplane, the talking machine, and the great American doughnut—well, almost, anyway. At least, the first working submarines that went places and did things—the grandfathers of the great undersea leviathans that pretty much control the seven seas today—were conceived, built, and manned by Americans.

DEFYING THE WHALE

To claim that the submarine is 100 per cent American in origin would be a bit extreme, because early, always interesting, but almost invariably unsuccessful experiments were made before America was even discovered. In fact, fragmentary records of submarine experiments go as far back as 1184 B.C., when, Aristotle states, some sort of diving-bell device was used at the Siege of Troy. And Alexander the Great is reputed to have "sat in a watertight bell and defied the whale"—whatever good that did.

Apparently this whale-defying effort consumed all such inventive talent for twenty-five centuries, for it was not until around A.D. 1400—still almost a century before America entered the picture—that a creative genius devised a submarine boat in the form of a cylinder with a detachable bow and stern. In outward appearance it probably bore a remote family resemblance to the submarine. It was designed to transport men across a river, but what happened to it, or to its successor—a "notable diving bell" devised in Toledo, Spain, in 1538 which had some of the more primitive attributes of a submarine—is a secret that has been lost in the mist of antiquity. In 1585 an Italian named Ganibelli partly destroyed a bridge near Antwerp with the use of small, low-lying boats loaded with gunpowder and set off with mechanisms; and the Dutch unloosed a fleet of submerged but uninhabited boats, set with time fuses, against the Spaniards. The boats were not submarines, to be sure, but they at least demonstrated the line of development that small torpedo-carrying craft would take. Even the talented Leonardo da Vinci at

7

The Rotterdam Boat

one time tried his hand at submarine designing.

All that we know for a certainty is that during these early centuries all the experiments were failures and that the geniuses who conceived them were looked upon as crackpots.

A RIDE FOR A KING

The first submarine really capable of carrying a human crew under water was invented by a Dutchman, Cornelius van Drebbel, in 1620—the very year the Pilgrims landed upon Plymouth Rock. His device was a rowboat, propelled by oars just like other rowboats, and so competently waterproofed by oiled leather and ventilated (by a secret method of revitalizing the air, which the inventor carried to his grave) that life could be sustained under water for several hours. In 1624 the inventor established his claim to fame by taking James I of England, his patron, on an underwater joyride.

Next followed a widely variant crew of submarine inventors, each of whom contributed his bit to the knowledge of underwater seafaring. There was the Frenchman de Son, for instance, who produced his "Rotterdam Boat" in 1652. This was of prodigious size—72 feet long, 12 feet wide, and 8 feet deep—and its main contribution to the art of submarining was a pair of hand-operated paddle wheels and a set of iron-tipped legs that permitted the craft to sit down on the river bottom when the crew got tired.

Perhaps the most significant early contribution was the use of leather bottles as ballast tanks. When the bottles were filled with water, the vessel submerged; when the water was forced out, the vessel surfaced. Those leather bottles

were the forerunners of the great ballast tanks on the modern submarines. This principle was applied in 1747 to the submarine contrived by Symons, an Englishman, whose vessel, like those of all his predecessors, was built of wood and powered by the conventional oars. An inventor named Borelli had conceived this principle of ballast as far back as 1680, but two generations had elapsed before the idea was given an actual test. It is not always easy to put the finger upon the inventor who was "first."

Then came the Americans. As the vision of undersea craft as instruments of war loomed and the American genius for invention swung into action, the submarine developed spectacularly. The first new arrival was David Bushnell.

Van Drebbel's Submarine

A YANKEE TURTLE

David Bushnell, born in Saybrook, Connecticut, in 1742, was as Yankee as the famed Connecticut nutmeg itself. Inflamed at the depredations of the British men-of-war along the New England coast, and perhaps inspired by the observation of Sir William Monson, one of Queen Elizabeth's admirals, that "a powerful ship is more easily sunk by an undersea shot than by ordinary gunfire," he concentrated his ingenuity upon proving to the Yale faculty that gunpowder would explode under water.

His next step was to build a strange contraption, which he did down at the "Ferry" in his own home town of Saybrook, at the mouth of the Connecticut, where flat-bottomed boats carried passengers across the river to what is now Old Lyme. There, with hammer and saw and chisel, he labored until he produced the first American submarine—and a weird craft it was. Its oaken hull was in the form of two shells like

8

the upper shell of a turtle, 7½ feet long and nearly as wide. Because of its close resemblance to the reptile from which the inventor obviously got his inspiration, the craft was known as the *American Turtle*. The crew consisted of one man, who operated the screw propeller — the first to be introduced into a submarine—with his feet. Enough air could be contained to keep the crew alive for about half an hour. Of course no lamps or candles could be carried, so phosphorus was used. This lighting system was suggested by no less an expert than Benjamin Franklin. Water, for use as ballast, was admitted through a valve at the bottom and was expelled by a couple of brass hand pumps. Above the rudder was the magazine, consisting of hollowed oak into which 150 pounds of gunpowder was packed; an inside mechanism set off the discharge at any time desired within twelve hours.

In April 1777, Bushnell notified Governor Trumbull: "Sir, I am prepared to blow up the entire British Navy."

Bushnell's *American Turtle*

THE TURTLE ATTACKS

The first attack was made upon Lord Howe's ship *Eagle,* sixty-four guns, lying off New York Harbor. Bushnell, himself too frail to manipulate the boat, selected one Sergeant Lee for the task. Under cover of darkness, Lee worked his way under the victim and tried to screw the powder magazine to the hull, where he proposed to leave it and make his escape. But pure chance intervened: the screw happened to hit a metal part of the hull and did not penetrate.

Upon leaving, Lee had to cast off the magazine, which was timed to set off the explosion in an hour. Though it went off as scheduled, the magazine had drifted too far from the victim to cause damage. But it threw the crew into terror.

So ended the first attack ever made by a submarine upon any warship. Though unsuccessful, it marked the beginning of underwater warfare.

Bushnell's next attempt on an enemy ship resulted in a peculiar accident. His intended victim was the British ship *Cerberus*, lying off New London. Again the magazine drifted loose from the hull, and floated under the eyes of the three sailors who constituted the crew of a captured schooner which the *Cerberus* had in tow. The sailors, assuming that the strange contrivance was a Yankee fishtrap of some kind, hauled it abroad. The schooner, crew and all, went to Davy Jones's locker—the first ship to fall a victim to submarine attack, even though by chance.

A later Bushnell effort was so devastating to the morale of the British sailors lying in the Delaware just above Philadelphia that it prompted the Revolutionary poet Francis Hopkinson to write his famous "Battle of the Kegs." A flock of underwater mines, modeled after the *American Turtle* but carrying no crews, was set adrift down the river among a fleet of British ships. Though only one schooner was sunk, the unexpected nature of the attack threw the enemy into such confusion over the "Yankee infernal machines" that the ships were hastily withdrawn to remote anchorages.

Fulton's *Nautilus*

FULTON'S FIRST "FOLLY"

The second American submarine inventor was Robert Fulton, who gave his underwater boat some resemblance to the submarine of to-day. Fulton, born in 1765, began his career as a miniature-painter. It was while he was studying art in Paris, along about 1800, that he developed the craft he called the *Nautilus*. This name the novelist Jules Verne subsequently applied to the fanciful submarine described in his *Twenty Thousand Leagues under the Sea,* which inspired a large circle of youthful inventors to bring that fanciful creation into actual being—and some of them actually did just that.

The Fulton boat was designed strictly for war purposes. Ovoid in shape, nearly 6 feet in diameter, it incorporated numerous advances over its predecessors; chief among them were reservoirs of compressed air which permitted longer submergence, tanks of water that permitted it to sink or rise at will, and horizontal planes. Sailing on the surface, Fulton was able to "furl sail, strike mast, and disappear beneath the water within two minutes."

This invention, together with the submarine mine and torpedo equipment that went with it, was vainly offered to the United States, to France, and to several other governments. The British government then gave Fulton a chance to demonstrate his goods in 1805. Using a 200-ton brig as his victim, he blew it up with 170 pounds of powder in a dramatic exhibition. It was the first vessel sunk by a submarine torpedo attack. "It made no more resistance than a bag of feathers, and went to pieces like a shattered egg," declared the inventor. Despite this performance, the British officers regarded the submarine with prophetic dislike and reported the Fulton boat to be impracticable, and the crestfallen inventor returned to Washington with his models and plans.

In 1807 he finally induced the United States government to back his experimental work, in the course of which he blew up a large brig in New York Harbor with a torpedo containing 70 pounds of powder. But the uncertainties and disappointments involved in dealing with politicians finally led Fulton into the field of steamboat navigation, where his fame lies secure.

NEW GAINS

The War of 1812 came and went without much progress in underwater fighting, although an American named Mix did make several attempts to blow up British vessels after the then-conventional manner of attaching a mine to the wooden hull of the victim by means of a submarine. He was followed by Captain Johnson, an Englishman, who in 1820 was somewhat more successful. Johnson was followed in turn by Wilhelm Bauer, of Germany, who built submarines for Germany that aided in breaking up the blockade of the Dutch fleet off Kiel (he also sold to Austria and Russia); by Le Brun, of France, who produced the *Plongeur,* which had the distinction of using compressed air for motive power for the first time; and by Monturiol, of Spain, whose *El Ictineo* won public acclaim but little else.

Then, with the Civil War in America, came a series of daring achievements with both submersibles and semisubmersibles employed by the Confederates (who had no navy of their own) against the warships of the Union.

Le Plongeur

The End of the *Hunley* and the *Housatonic*

CHAPTER II
Submersibles in the Civil War

O F THE submersibles—the real submarines —the Confederates built three. The first was the *Pioneer,* constructed by private capital in 1862. Though only 20 feet long, it embodied numerous advances in submarine design and was a product of true craftsmanship. Fabricated of quarter-inch iron sheets, motivated by a propeller operated by two men, and equipped with bow and stern rudders and side vanes, it gave an excellent performance during its trials by blowing up a barge placed as a target. But when it set forth to challenge the flagship of Admiral Farragut when he started up the Mississippi in 1862 to capture New Orleans, the *Pioneer* became unmanageable for reasons which will never be known, and mysteriously sank with all hands. Found by accident years later, the boat is now on view in New Orleans as "The world's only privateer submarine."

THE SUICIDE CLUB

The second of the Confederate submarines foundered before it ever saw service. But the third, the *Hunley,* had a career as tempestuous and as tragic as any that ever ended in a burst of glory. Her ship's complement consisted of one officer and eight men. Her designed purpose was to navigate submerged under an enemy ship, towing a torpedo on a 200-foot line. The *Hunley,* or *Boat Fish,* as it was commonly called, was to rise beyond the ship just as the timed torpedo blew it up. It seemed like a good idea, but during the trials she went out of control and plunged headlong into the mud of Mobile Bay, where her crew was suffocated. Her next trial was made in Charleston, where a volunteer crew once more sacrificed their lives in the same way, only two men escaping. The vessel was nicknamed the "Peripatetic Coffin," but in spite of this gruesome reminder of her record a third crew volunteered and died similarly; so did a fourth crew, and a fifth. Then the *Hunley* was converted into a semisubmersible of the *David* type to carry on. Certainly the sons of the South were not lacking in valor; the names of those who had enrolled in this suicide club, at least all of the names that are known, are now written in bronze on a tablet in Charleston.

The *Davids* (named after David Bushnell or after the David who slew Goliath, according to which school of thought one belongs to) were almost submarines, but not quite. They ran nearly submerged but, because they were propelled by steam, they had to have a funnel, which stuck out of the water at their sterns; when prepared for attack, these funnels were drawn in to lie nearly level with the water. Their bows were fitted with copper torpedoes loaded with 60 pounds of gunpowder, at the end of 22-foot booms.

The first of the tribe appeared in Charleston Harbor on the evening of October 5, 1863.

Leaning over the rail of the formidable ironclad, the *New Ironsides,* the officer of the deck peered curiously at what appeared to be a wide board floating toward the ship.

"What does that look like to you?" he inquired of his mate.

"Looks like a covered rowboat smoking a big cigar," was the reply.

"Ahoy, there!" called the watch.

The answer was the discharge of a shotgun that sent the officer down in a pool of blood. This was followed by a terrific upheaval that almost laid the ironclad on her beam ends. The floating board was a *David,* and she had all but accomplished her mission. She did not sink the *New Ironsides,* but she did send her to the docks for several months of repair work.

This was the first instance in which the underwater menace had deliberately gone on the prowl for warships, and the near success of the effort inspired the Confederacy to experiment further. It was then that the submarine *Hunley* was converted into a semisubmersible *David,* equipped with a torpedo at the end of a long spar, and sent out to get a Union "Goliath" in the North Channel. On the night of February 17, 1864, she approached the *U.S.S. Housatonic.* For a moment the officer of the deck hesitated; perhaps the strange object in the water was only a board after all. Then he sounded the alarm. The engines were put into reverse, but before the ship could gain momentum it was ripped asunder, and sank in five minutes— the first warship ever to be sunk by a submarine. The *Hunley* was destroyed along with its vic-

tim. Every member of its sixth crew went to his doom. The *Hunley* is probably the only vessel to have lost practically 600 per cent of its crew.

HALF A CENTURY OF EXPERIMENT

The *Housatonic* was both the first and the last warship to be destroyed by a submarine until the outbreak of the first World War in 1914. But during that fifty-year interval a great deal of progress was being quietly made in the development of the submarine by two nations (or more accurately, by the inventors of two nations) that could visualize the future of war beneath the waves—the United States and France. Both of these nations pursued their experiments independently of each other. Both were obviously influenced by the historic battle between the Confederate ironclad ram *Merrimac* and the new type of Union ironclad, the *Monitor,* on March 9, 1862—a battle that changed the whole course of naval warfare in general and of submarine warfare in particular.

The introduction of the ironclad was a knockout blow to the tenaciously held theory that the function of a submarine was to glide under the hull of its enemy and screw a mine to its wooden hull. Even as late as 1865 the American inventor Halstead persistently clung to this ancient doctrine and produced a unique submarine appropriately called *The Intelligent Whale* which contained a water lock that enabled a diver to step out of the vessel and attach a mine to the steel hull of the enemy by means of rubber suction pads and other devices. But none of these ingenious ideas worked successfully in practice.

Meanwhile in quick succession came two innovations that set the submarine squarely upon the course of development it has pursued ever since. One was the construction by the French in 1863 of the first all-steel submarine, a 146-foot vessel that operated with an 80-horsepower engine. The second was the invention of the Whitehead torpedo in 1864 by an Englishman —the first automatically propelled torpedo that operated on compressed air.

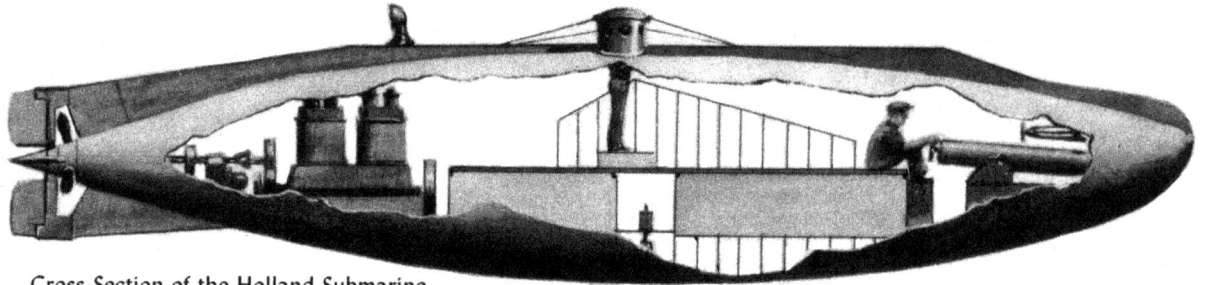

Cross-Section of the Holland Submarine

CHAPTER III

The Modern Submarine Gradually Emerges

URING the generation following the Civil War inventors of assorted nationalities kept at work on the submarine. Each contributed his bit to the steadily accumulating fund of knowledge about undersea warfare.

There was James Nasmyth, the Englishman, whose experiments began in 1855 with a steam engine equipped with a high-pressure boiler that drove his submarine over the water at a 10-knot clip. His work led the way for more intensive experimentation with steam by Otto Vogel of Germany, in 1869, and later, in 1883, by Alstitt the American, who used both steam and electricity.

There was the Frenchman Claude Goubert, who between 1878 and 1890 carried forward the earlier work of the French Professor Marié-Davy on a propeller driven by electric power. Incidentally he produced the first periscope, a stubby affair as immobile as a telephone pole, which ran up through the conning tower.

There was Gustave Zédé, who designed the famous *Gymnote* submarine, which on electric power went under the water at the rate of 7 or 8 knots. A unique but unsuccessful feature of his craft was its method of carrying torpedoes in drop collars.

There was the American inventor Mortensen, who produced the first submarine with a torpedo tube in its bow—a feature which was further developed by T. V. Nordenfeldt, of Sweden, and G. W. Garret, of England. All of them helped

to lay the groundwork for the present-day undersea craft.

There was Woodhouse, an Englishman, who as early as 1881 strove to propel submarines by compressed air. There was D'Allest, the Frenchman, who in 1886 fitted up a submarine with an oil-combustion engine, while Drzewiecki, the Russian, was experimenting with the new electric motors. There were Genoud, whose hobby was a gas engine worked by hydrogen, and Blakesley, who in 1884 proposed to use steam raised in a sort of fireless boiler heated by a chemical composition. There were the New York professor, Josiah Tuck, and the Chicagoan, George C. Baker, whose boat submerged by side propellers which could be inclined up or down.

And there was Romazzetti, the Frenchman, who about 1893 produced the first submarine with a double hull—the forerunner of the double hulls used today. Nor would the list be complete without mention of Bourgeous and Brun, who produced steel reservoirs of compressed air at a pressure of at least 15 atmospheres or about 210 pounds per square inch—a principle that was adopted later by the famous American John P. Holland and by his contemporary Simon Lake.

THE U. S. NAVY ORDERS A SUBMARINE

During this period, of course, the Navy was keeping a watchful but skeptical eye upon the submarine inventors here at home. Some of them had been undertaking peculiar experi-

13

DEATH IN THE NIGHT

The "ears" of the Nazi submarine, its powerful listening devices, located this loaded tanker after it had left a large oil installation along the U. S. coast. The men hurried to "battle stations," a torpedo was launched, and now the submarine has surfaced to finish off the job with its deck guns.

ments, under foreign patronage, that were threatening to cause international complications. Uncle Sam did not look upon these newfangled schemes for waging war underseas with any marked degree of warmth. As one high-ranking official expressed it: "No one but a crazy man would waste his time inventing a submarine and no one but a lunatic would go down in it if it were invented."

Not until Uncle Sam was confronted with the possibility of war with England over the Venezuela affair during the second administration of Grover Cleveland (1893-97) did Congress awaken to the low estate into which our Navy had been allowed to fall because of lack of funds; then it came suddenly to life and voted $200,000 for experimental submarine construction. Mindful of the appalling fatality rate among the Confederate submersibles, the Secretary of the Navy hesitated to issue a formal order that might jeopardize many human lives unduly.

"How do we know," he asked, "that life can endure on a submerged vessel if an explosion, such as a mine or torpedo, occurs near it?"

To find the answer to this question, the first official test of underwater craft ever made under the auspices of the United States Navy was ordered, and a memorable experiment it was, with as odd a crew as ever sailed in a Navy vessel. A cat, a rooster, a rabbit, and a dove were placed aboard a miniature submersible (a watertight tank) and set adrift. Then a series of submarine explosions of guncotton were set off at decreasing ranges. When the last explosion was completed, at a distance of 100 feet, the submersible was brought ashore and the strange assortment of shipmates examined. The dove and the rabbit had died, but the cat and the rooster were not only alive but indignant and articulate. As a result of this reassuring demonstration the Navy, in 1895, invited bids for the building of a submarine. The cat and the rooster had changed the course of our naval history.

THE SUBMARINE FINDS ITS GENIUS

In response to the Navy's first call, in 1895,

eight bids were submitted, and for the first time the government was able to get a survey of the progress that had been made in submarine design. The occasion brought two American inventors into the limelight. One was Simon Lake, whose spectacular underwater experiments brought him contracts from other nations but never one from his own. The other was John P. Holland, who won the United States government contract and from whose inventive genius the fighting submarine of today has grown.

Simon Lake began his career with a dream of a submarine, patterned after the Jules Verne conception, that would explore the bottom of the sea, salvage sunken treasure, and eventually carry cargoes under water across the oceans. With the aid of relatives he built his first boat,

The Argonaut

the *Argonaut Junior,* a 14-foot pitch-pine affair with a propeller operated by a man-power crank and a compressed-air reservoir that was a "tank from a bankrupt soda fountain," and a pump that had "begun life as a plumber's hand pump." The contrivance was equipped with wheels with which she made her first underwater trip across the Shrewsbury River and back, in New Jersey. This effort was followed by the *Argonaut* in 1897, which had not only wheels but an air-lock compartment which enabled occupants to pick up objects from the bottom and even to spear fish. So fascinating was this feature to a party of twenty-seven guests selected from the leading citizens of Bridgeport, Connecticut, that each one insisted upon experiencing the wonders of this air chamber for himself. Thus the underwater pleasure trip in the Sound extended so long after the time scheduled for the return that the vessel was met at the dock by a panic-stricken populace who had already summoned the wrecking barges and prepared the obituary notices for the local papers.

Lake's interests focused on the development of the "level-keel" type of submarine, which could submerge while maintaining an even keel, as compared to the "diving" types, and he introduced two sets of hydroplanes for maintaining submergence at the desired depth—a system of controlled submergence now being used.

THE IRISH IN SUBMARINES

To the old-line Navy man the name "Holland" has been so intimately tied up with submarines that the two words are practically synonymous. The story of the American undersea craft is interwoven with the life of a boy who was born in a seaport town in Ireland in 1842, amid the sufferings of the years of famine. Holland, while still a young schoolteacher, fled to the United States with bitterness in his heart and a burning impulse to keep open the path to Irish freedom by challenging the power of Britannia's navy. This he intended to do by means of Lilliputian underwater craft which, he figured, could be used to great advantage by a weaker naval power against a stronger—a doctrine that history was destined to demonstrate.

Even as a schoolboy he had conceived of himself as a knight-errant; his first set of plans for the submarine that he proposed to use as his weapon were laid when he was barely seventeen. But it was not until 1877 that funds contributed by Irish associates enabled the youthful inventor to build the first Holland submarine. It was launched in the humble Passaic River, New Jersey, amid the clatter of silk factories and the hum of machine shops. It was a cigar-shaped affair, 10 feet long, operated by one man, and its sketchy motive power was furnished by a boiler made from a beer keg and toted on a steam launch that trailed along behind. Nevertheless, the strange contraption did run on the surface and it did make short dives, and once it stayed under water for twenty-four hours, with its inventor inside, just to show that it could.

As the result of these amazing performances, more money was forthcoming from the same sources. Holland's second submarine, built in 1881, was unofficially but significantly known as the *Fenian Ram*. The name, coined by a newspaperman, was derived from the Fenians, a militant group of Irishmen who were then beginning to visualize a fleet of submarines to prey upon British shipping. The *Fenian Ram* was 30 feet long, displaced 17 tons gross, cost $13,000, and took two years to build; altogether it was probably the most promising if not exactly the most formidable craft of its kind created up to that time, and it caused an enormous amount of speculation. Before its defects (chief of which was an engine that did not work) could be corrected, the contentious Irish broke into a quarrel among themselves and the *Fenian Ram* was ingloriously stolen, never to reappear.

But it marked a turning point in Holland's career. Years later, when the havoc that the *Fenian Rams* proposed to wreak upon British shipping was accomplished by other powers on a breath-taking scale, the Irish boasted that without their aid Holland could not have gone ahead, the submarine might never have been made a practical weapon, and the whole course of history might have been changed. If the Irish question did not exactly launch the modern submarine, it did give it something of a push.

THE SUBMARINE JOINS THE NAVY

The next step forward was made possible by the co-operation of an Army officer, Edward Zalinski, whose inventive genius at the time was concentrated upon his pneumatic dynamite torpedo gun. Realizing how closely both Holland's invention and his own entered into the same field, Zalinski organized a corporation for Holland in 1886. It produced a 50-foot submarine which incorporated several new devices; not the least of them was a pneumatic gun for firing a large dynamite charge. When within a mile of the target, the bow would be brought to the surface and the shell fired, and the boat would then submerge again. But the Zalinski boat was injured beyond repair during her launching.

For a few years Holland dropped out of public view. Not until he won the contract for building the first American Navy submarine, at a price of $150,000, was the inventor enabled to set his talents to work again.

The vessel built under this contract was named the *Plunger,* and with it the inventor got his first bitter experience with governmental officialdom, which insisted that every item be submitted to "experts" for approval. The boat was 85 feet long, displaced 168 tons, and was armed with two torpedo tubes; but when steam engines specified and insisted upon by the government engineers had been installed it became so overheated that no crew could live within it and it was never able to leave its dock.

Having expected just this failure, Holland pleaded that he be permitted to build his next model according to his own plans, unhampered by red tape and governmental interference—and at his own expense. This submarine, the sixth built by the inventor, was the famous *Holland.* It was 54 feet long, with a displacement of 74 tons submerged, was equipped with two horizontal diving rudders, and was propelled on the surface by a 50-horsepower gasoline engine and under water by electricity. After a heartbreaking series of trials and misadventures and adjustments that extended over four years, during which Holland leaned heavily upon his chief engineer and captain, Frank T. Cable, the Navy finally gave it the O.K., and on April 18, 1900, the vessel was purchased for the contract price

of $150,000, which was less than two-thirds of what it cost the company to build it. Thus the United States Navy got its first submarine.

THE RACE BEGINS

The acquisition of the *Holland* was followed by an order from the Navy for six more submarines of an improved type, at a cost of $170,000 each. Because one of them was named the *Adder,* all of this group was listed as the "Adder class," and bore the official numbers A-1 to A-7 inclusive. These seven vessels constituted Uncle Sam's first submarine flotilla.

Japan laid the basis for her submarine force with the purchase of five Holland boats in 1900; the British followed with the purchase of five vessels from Holland in 1901. In 1904 both Holland and Lake sold submarines to Russia. The Italians, who had quietly but successfully been developing submarines since 1889, then began to join the procession. The French, whose progress in submarine construction was extensive, had already attained a commanding position in the field. Neither France nor Italy, however, made effective use of their underwater craft during the World War of 1914-18, nor has France figured in World War II. Ironically enough, Germany, which was destined to make the greatest use of this weapon, was the last of the powers to become interested in underwater warfare; indeed, she did not build her first submarine until 1908—only six years before World War I began. It was built on the Holland principle, but later this was discarded for the *Germania* class built by the Krupps.

The fight for underwater supremacy was now under way.

The Adder

Hersing Spots the *Pathfinder*

CHAPTER IV

The Test of the Submarine in War

O N A blustery morning in August 1914—only a few days after the war had burst upon a stunned world—young Lieutenant Otto Hersing of the Imperial German Navy was scanning the horizon from the bridge of his submarine, the *U-21*. It was one of the twelve new and as yet untried German undersea fighters which had been ordered into the North Sea to hunt Allied warships and to attack them with torpedoes. Never before had German submarines been ordered into action; the assignment was, therefore, something in the nature of a test. Germany's submarine flotilla at the time was barely six years old and consisted of only eighteen serviceable vessels of 250 tons each, manned by small crews of twenty and using kerosene for fuel.

FIRST BLOOD

Off in the distance the young skipper spotted a trail of black smoke. Taking no chances, he sounded the alarm. Every man rushed to his diving station.

"All clear for diving," the engineer reported to the conning tower.

"Flood!" commanded Hersing. As his craft submerged to periscope depth, he took his position at the eyepiece of the instrument. The distant vessel was coming in his direction; the U-boat needed merely to lie in wait for it. As the stranger approached, the U-boat commander could get but fleeting glimpses of her big guns through the waves; by the same token, the "white water" served as an excellent screen to the periscope: it would even conceal the wake of the torpedo.

At short range, 500 yards or so, the torpedo was launched. It hit the warship squarely, below the water line and just under the forward funnel. With a mighty roar that was heard for miles, the fatally wounded ship burst into flames, her forward section shattered beyond hope. Rearing her stern high into the air, she took a nose dive into the depths. Within three minutes all was over. She was the first warship to fall prey to an undersea fighter since the destruction of the

U.S.S. Housatonic in the Civil War, fifty years before. She was the British light cruiser *Pathfinder,* 5,000 tons, with a complement of 268 officers and men—about half of whom were saved.

NEW PREY FOR THE SUBMARINE

Within a few weeks—on October 20, 1914, to be exact—another U-boat commander, Lieutenant Feldkirchner of the *U-17,* scored another fateful "first" when he captured and sank the British merchantman *Glystra,* loaded with contraband, by opening her sea cocks. This action was fraught with deep significance in the light of later events. It was taken upon the initiative of the submarine commander, who had exceeded his instructions; he had been ordered merely to attack warships. Because he was not equipped with prize lists, contraband regulations, or other items required for a campaign against mercantile craft, he reached his home port in the justified fear of a court-martial. The commander-in-chief, however, approved the act. More than that, it gave the German High Command an idea: why not wage a war against Allied shipping and blockade England just as England was blockading Germany?

Within a few days Germany's undersea fighters were handed formal instructions pertaining to contraband, prize crews, and rules of conduct. This measure was followed by formal orders to destroy enemy shipping.

The first Allied merchantman to fall prey to German submarines as the direct result of the order to destroy Allied shipping was the French ship *Malachite.* It was sunk by the *U-21*—the same vessel that sank the *Pathfinder.*

Thus was born, from incidents of minor importance in themselves, an epoch-making naval policy. The submarine was making good with a bang.

A RECORD VICTORY

The outstanding and certainly the most dramatic single act of a submarine during the World War—and since then, for that matter—

was performed by the *U-9,* commanded by the famed Lieutenant Otto Weddigen. It happened in the North Sea on September 22, 1914, a day when the water was as smooth as the conventional glass and the visibility excellent. The *U-9* was resting on the surface, recharging its batteries, when three British armored cruisers of the 12,000-ton class were sighted. Half-crippled, with its batteries only partly charged, the *U-9* submerged. When it was within 500 yards of the first cruiser, a torpedo was launched — so close that the submarine dived deep in order to minimize the expected concussion upon itself. In 31 seconds the missile had struck and the sound of the explosion had traveled back to the U-boat. Rising quickly to take a peep through the periscope at the results of the attack, Weddigen saw the stricken vessel sinking by the stern, her four stacks blowing off steam and her lifeboats being frantically manned. It was *H.M.S. Aboukir.*

Her two companions stood bravely but unwisely by, to rescue the victims—a tactical blunder that, by official orders, was not repeated again. The *U-9* approached to within 300 yards of her second quarry and unleashed two torpedoes at a range too short to miss. This time the victim was *H.M.S. Hogue.* "She seemed to give one jump right out of the water and go straight down," reported an eyewitness.

By this time the sea was strewn with wreckage, lifeboats, and struggling men. Using its last torpedoes, the *U-9* attacked the third ship. The impact of the explosion turned the cruiser completely over on her side, and within a few minutes she too—*H.M.S. Cressy*—was gone.

The whole sensational episode, in which a single small submarine destroyed 36,000 tons of warships, and 1,370 officers and men out of a total of about 2,250, had occupied less than an hour.

THE ALLIES STRIKE BACK

The early successes of the U-boats were not surprising. Great Britain and her allies had vast numbers of merchant vessels on the high seas,

The Sinking of the *Prinz Adalbert*

whereas Germany had practically none. Moreover, the German Navy kept discreetly in hiding, while the Allied warships were roaming everywhere. Thus the U-boats were presented with innumerable targets, and that they took advantage of the situation was evidenced by the appalling losses they inflicted upon their enemies. Only on rare occasions did a British submarine catch a German warship at large, and when it did it performed as effectively as its German counterparts. When the British submarine *E-8,* for example, happened upon the German 9,000-ton cruiser *Prinz Adalbert* in the Baltic on October 23, 1915, it fired a torpedo that set off the enemy's magazine, and the destruction of the vessel was reported to be "so instantaneous and complete" that not a single survivor was found.

The British submarines that so gallantly entered the Dardanelles against tremendous technical difficulties and hazards, not the least of which were mine fields, tortuous turns, and heavy currents, inflicted enormous damage on the Turkish supply, cargo, and troop ships. One of the most conspicuous feats was performed by the *B-11,* an obsolescent little craft commanded by Lieutenant Norman Holbrook, which torpedoed the Turkish battleship *Messudiyeh*—an act that won the young submarine commander the Victoria Cross. Not long afterward Commander Courtney Boyle, of the British submarine *E-11,*

adroitly picked his way into the Sea of Marmora and blew up the last of the Turkish battleships, the *Barbarossa.*

On the rare occasions when the German High Seas Fleet ventured out, British submarines did their job. The only two German dreadnoughts to risk themselves outside of Kiel after the Battle of Jutland were both torpedoed by submarines on the same day. They compensated in part for the loss, by submarine attack, of the British battleships *Triumph, Majestic, Formidable, Cornwallis,* and finally the *Britannia*—the last of England's Goliaths to go down before the Davids of the U-boat flotilla. She was destroyed by the last torpedo unleashed in the war.

THE MENACE GROWS

The submarine had introduced an immensely formidable weapon into naval warfare; the undersea fighters had established their usefulness on an unprecedented scale. For nearly three years the Allies were practically helpless before the onslaught of the U-boats. No effective defense was devised against them. Allied losses soared to alarming heights, in some cases as high as 1,000,000 tons of shipping a month. (The total ships produced by the United States even during the emergency year 1941 aggregated a bare 1,100,000 tons.) During the first seventeen months of the war, only twenty-four U-boats were disposed of by the British, and all of them were sunk by the conventional and century-old methods employed against surface vessels—by gunfire and by ramming. The first submarine to be destroyed by ramming was the *U-15,* which was ridden down by the British cruiser *Birmingham* in the early weeks of the conflict; the British battleship *Dreadnought* similarly eliminated the *U-29,* with the loss of all hands, including the famous Lieutenant Weddigen.

True, the British did make sporadic efforts to meet the U-boat crisis. Their first big invention was the Q-ship, the "mystery" vessel that pretended to be a humble freighter but in reality was heavily armed. Under the direction of the daring Gordon Campbell, V.C., the flotilla, which eventually totaled 180 Q-ships, disposed of fourteen U-boats before the ruse was discovered and the Q-ships themselves began sinking under U-boat attacks.

Steel nets, laid by fishing vessels, were used to entangle submarines, but they proved to be more of a nuisance than a menace, and the damage done by them was inconsiderable. Even mine fields proved less effective than was expected—until the Americans entered the war in 1917 and began laying mines on a scale that astounded the entire world. Airplanes were used for attacking submarines, but they carried such light bombs (most of them only ten-pounders) that even when they scored hits the damage was trifling. The Germans used both airplanes and Zeppelins, but neither wrought much havoc; indeed, a Zeppelin was even captured by the British submarine *E-31* on May 4, 1916, and its crew taken prisoner. On another occasion the British submarine *C-25* successfully stood off an attack by five German seaplanes at once. Not until the Americans came in 1917 were effective measures taken to curb the terrific toll exacted by the U-boats.

By February 1917 the submarine had driven Great Britain to desperation; she was literally fighting for her very survival. "Could Germany have kept fifty submarines constantly at work on the great shipping routes in the winter and spring of 1917," stated Admiral Sims, the commander-in-chief of the American Naval Forces, "nothing could have prevented her from winning the war." Information concerning the critical situation had been withheld from the British people. By April 1917 only a month's supply of food remained in England; she was confronted with the specter of famine. "The Germans will win unless we stop these losses and stop them soon" was the startling admission made to Admiral Sims by the British Admiral Jellicoe. The submarine, more than any other factor in the World War, had brought the British Empire to her knees.

THE TIDE TURNS

Then on April 7, 1917, the United States entered the war. Immediately the picture was changed. Mine fields were laid on a scale that the British had believed impossible. The convoy system was inaugurated. Depth charges were devised. And the combination of these factors marked the beginning of the end of the U-boat war. During the final sixteen months that the United States was in the war, far more U-boats were destroyed than had been sunk by all the Allied navies combined during the three years preceding.

The box score at the finish disclosed that British submarines had sunk 54 enemy warships and 274 other vessels, and that a total of 178 U-boats had been destroyed (according to the German figures) by the following means:

Depth charges, patrols, etc.	53
Unknown causes	33
Mines	20
Ramming	19
Enemy submarines	19
Decoy ships	14
Diving mishaps, accidents	9
Net barrages	6
Aircraft	5

The necessity of devising ways to protect the submarine from the anti-submarine methods that grew out of the World War forced the next step in the development of the submarine.

The C-25 Rides Out the Storm

A Destroyer Dumps Its Ashcans

CHAPTER V

Enemies That Stalk the Submarine

IN TARGET PRACTICE the success of the 1910 model of submarines against surface craft was so startling as to inspire naval chieftains to make a study of defensive measures against them. The first anti-submarine committee appointed by the British Admiralty emerged from an early session with the ingenious if somewhat primitive idea that an enemy submarine could be stalked by a picket boat, the periscope lassoed, and an explosive charge slid down to blow a hole in the hull. Tying sponges over the periscope and focusing searchlights upon it to blind the officer below were other gems considered, but the crowning suggestion was to train seals to locate and follow underwater craft. Two seals, Queenie and Lizzie, were actually kept muzzled and fed only from a submarine, to build up the association between food and submarines. Just what the procedure was to be will never be known because the training was never completed. Perhaps the experimenters were unable to find the answer to an analogous problem propounded by Abraham Lincoln as he watched a small dog furiously chase a passing railroad train:

"What do you suppose," he inquired, "that dog would do with that train if he caught it?"

SAUCE FOR THE GANDER

Along about 1914, however, howitzers, bomb-throwing devices, and explosive paravanes (devices for removing mines in the paths of warships) came into use. From these have developed the anti-submarine weapons in use today.

The arch enemies of the submarines are destroyers, airplanes, and fast little PC boats (submarine-chasers). The latter are of two types: 100 feet and 170 feet; and they are armed with machine guns, three-inch guns, and depth charges. The principal anti-submarine weapon of both the destroyer and the airplane, and incidentally of the PC boat, is the depth bomb, also called "depth charge" or "ashcan." The British are using "corvettes" for patrol and convoy duty as well.

The standard depth bomb comes in the form

of a metal drum that carries anywhere from 200 or 300 to 600 pounds of T.N.T. These drums are "set" to explode at any desired depth; the mechanism is automatically put in motion by the pressure of the water. Normally they are set to explode at about 80 feet, although this may be varied from 30 feet to 300 feet. Any submarine within 100 feet of such an explosion is due for a jolt that may well be its last. Evidence of a hit comes in the form of oil bubbles and sometimes debris that rises to the surface. One of the tricks of the submarine to discourage further pursuit is to play dead—to simulate destruction by the release of oil and bubbles. That is why so many reports come of "submarines supposed to have been sunk." Oil and bubbles on the surface are not proof.

As soon as a destroyer locates a submarine, or thinks it has, the ordinary procedure is to charge at full speed toward the spot and run circles around it at increasing distances, dropping a depth bomb barrage all the while. As the speed of a destroyer is officially stated to be "only 35 knots" (though unofficially it is known to be a great deal faster than that), and as the underwater speed of a submarine varies from only 6 to 11 knots, the chase resolves itself into a matching of wits tempered with a trace of luck.

DUMPING THE ASHCANS

The mechanism for releasing these depth charges is simplicity itself. A quantity of the drums are loaded on to a metal framework with inclined tracks leading over the stern. The drums are released one at a time, by a simple twist of the wrist; the force of gravity rolls them off the inclined plane into the ship's wake. And the ship had better be going right along, too—25 knots or more—if she hopes to avoid the repercussion that follows in a few seconds and sends a mountain of water into the air.

Another device for discharging these drums is known as the "Y-gun," so-called because it is shaped like the letter Y, with two barrels, three feet long and branching off at a 90-degree angle.

One charge of powder at the juncture of the two barrels hurls two 300-pound depth charges simultaneously, one from each side of the ship. The guns have a range of about 30 yards.

The use of airplanes not only for spotting submarines but also for dropping special depth bombs upon them is one of the latest innovations of the present war. Naturally enough, the mechanisms employed are not being widely publicized, but that they are effective was aptly indicated in the terse radiogram report sent to the Navy Department early in 1942 by one of the Navy fliers:

"Sighted sub. Sank same."

Perhaps the most common question asked by Mr. John Q. Citizen of the fliers who hunt submarines is: "How far under the water can you see a boat from the air?" The answer is that old favorite: "It all depends." In the muddy waters such as are found around some of our cities a submarine is barely visible 10 feet below the surface, while an airplane photograph made over the crystal-clear waters of the tropics may show a submarine in detail apparently on the surface when actually it is submerged 100 feet.

SLEEPING DYNAMITE

Another plot against the peace of mind of the submarine's crew is the mine field. The standard submarine mine is spherical in shape, about three feet in diameter, and packs a wallop that only 300 pounds of T.N.T. can give. It may be anchored at any desired depth; usually the mines are laid not only in overlapping rows but also at varying levels, ranging from 45 to 240 feet. A submarine need not actually hit a mine to cause a detonation; it need merely come into contact with any one of its antenna wires, which radiate 50 feet outward and are known as "magnetic pistols." These must not be confused with the so-called "magnetic mines" devised by the Germans as the mysterious "secret weapon" that would mow down their foes. These magnetic mines explode without direct contact; they are detonated by the magnetic disturbance caused by the mere proximity of the metal mass of the vessel passing over its delicate mechanisms. The method now being used for counteracting this threat is a dark naval secret—but the newspapers do refer occasionally to "demagnetizing cables" that encircle the ships, like a magic girdle or talisman, to prevent the vessels from falling under the spell of these twentieth-century Germanic sirens.

THE SUBMARINE'S WORST ENEMY

Curiously enough, one of the most effective enemies of a submarine is any enemy submarine. At the present time certain undersea craft are assigned exclusively to the task of hunting down their own kind. They know each other's habits; they can sense "what the other fellow would do —if." They know, for instance, that submarines must fix their positions at intervals, and come up within sighting distance of certain headlands. At such localities the hunter lies in wait for his prey, and the mortality rate in the general neighborhood of such navigational marks is high. The hunters also lie in wait for enemy submarines off such well-defined points as are usually passed by merchant vessels. A submarine on the surface, too, is more quick to detect a periscope than any other type of vessel is; it is quicker to detect, through its secret listening devices, the noises made by other submarines. Submarines are so conscious of each other's presence that they do not like to surface in alien waters and thus expose themselves to attack.

"In proportion to the various types of antisubmarine craft employed," was the surprising statement of Admiral Sims following the World War of 1914-18, "Allied submarines sank three times as many submarines as Allied destroyers and twenty times as many as auxiliary patrol craft."

New kinds of weapons and new uses of old ones all contribute to the surprise factor in warfare. Small Navy blimps, for example, are not new, but their value as spotters of hostile submarines has been suddenly noticed and has put them in high favor. Submarine nets are not new, but now their uses are being greatly extended: cables reaching to the ocean floor and intertwined on floats now guard every important harbor in the country. Among the surprises, you will remember, sprung on the submarines during the last war were the mystery ships, or "Q-ships," used by the British against the German U-boats. To outward appearances these Q-ships were nothing more than small, ordinary tramp steamers, and none-too-smart ones at that, manned by ill-trained civilian crews; actually they were manned by skilled Navy men especially trained in the use of cleverly concealed guns. When the U-boat surfaced and gave the crew of its victim time to escape before the doomed vessel was sunk by gunfire, the inoffensive old tramp steamer suddenly blazed into action and sank the submarine before it could submerge. When the ruse became generally known, the submarines played safe and did not surface at all. They used their torpedoes instead.

SPOTTING THE SUBMARINE

How is the presence of a submarine detected? The best method is actually to see a submarine on the surface or in the act of diving. Next to that is to catch a glimpse of a periscope; one may have to look quickly to see this, as periscopes are warily raised only for fleeting glimpses when in hostile waters. Another way to detect it is by the hum of its motors as heard on the listening gear; such telltale noises may be heard in broad daylight when no vessel is even in sight. Another way is to spot a streak of oil upon the water. Still another is to catch sight of air bubbles that arise when the boat is diving, or, even better, to catch a flash of the wake made by its propellers. Perhaps the most dangerous clue the submarine gives of its whereabouts is the telltale bubbles that come up when a torpedo is discharged—a most inopportune moment in which to give one's position away. The inventor who thinks up a scheme for eradicating this mark has a big niche awaiting him in the Navy's Hall of Fame.

A SWIFT VENGEANCE

Here are submarine hunters in action! A shore patrol blimp spied a surfaced Nazi submarine raider attacking a defenseless coastwise steamer. The blimp radioed its find to shore, and a Navy dive bomber was dispatched to the spot. Now the dive bomber has "laid its eggs"—and the Nazi submarine is starting on its last dive.

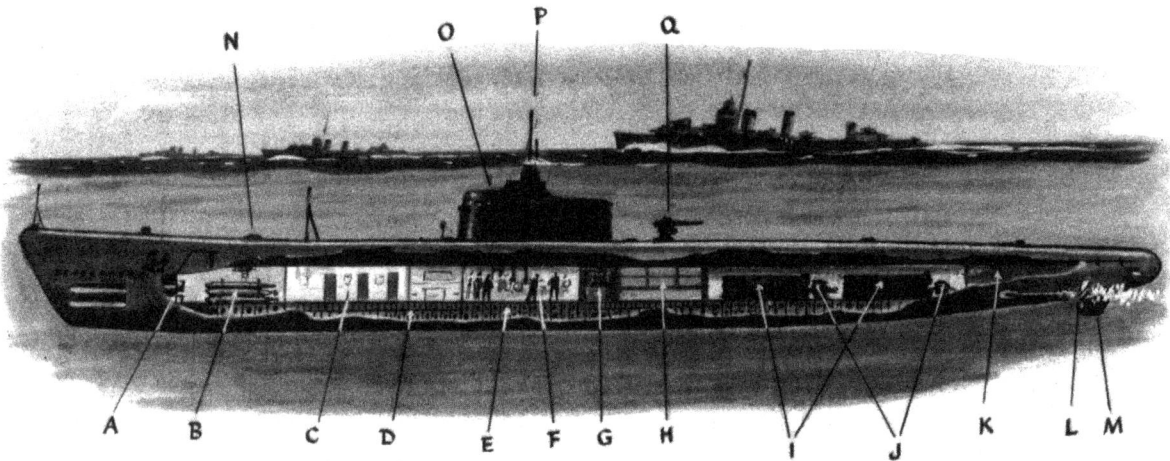

Modern American Submarine, Showing: A torpedo tubes, B torpedoes, C officers' quarters, D storage batteries, E ballast and fuel tanks, F control room, G galley, H crew's quarters, I Diesel engines, J electric motors, K torpedo room, L propellers, M rudder, N escape hatch, O conning tower, P periscope, Q deck gun.

CHAPTER VI

How the Modern Submarine Is Designed

IT IS ALWAYS thrilling to see the surface of the sea unexpectedly broken by the slim finger of a rising periscope, friend or foe, cutting the water like a knife and leaving behind it a thin, feathery wake. As the water-swept conning tower emerges, its picturesque silhouette suggests the dripping battlements and towers of the legendary island of Atlantis, mysteriously rising from the depths.

A HUNDRED YARDS OF SHIP

When it rests on the surface, so little of a submarine is seen above the water line that the ship looks shorter and more fashionably slender than she really is. Actually, the over-all underwater length of the type of submarine that Uncle Sam is building today is about 320 feet—longer than a football field. Her slim, narrow deck at its widest part amidships is barely 15 feet, and it tapers off to a point both fore and aft. Below the top deck, however, she bulges out into a fat hull which ranges from 26 to 30 feet across the beam, and which, in cross section, is about circular, in order better to withstand the water pressure. Between the outer hull and the inner (or "pressure" hull, as it is called) are the ballast tanks. The gradual increase in size of American submarines from the *Holland,* with its modest 54-foot length and its 74-ton displacement, reached its climax in the mine-laying submarine *Argonaut* in 1928, with its 381-foot length and 4,000-ton displacement. The cruiser submarines *Narwhal* and *Nautilus* were not far behind. Since then, however, the trend had been toward somewhat smaller vessels which can be more effectively maneuvered.*

NAMING THE PIG BOATS

No longer are Uncle Sam's submarines identified impersonally by mere alphabetical and numerical symbols, after the manner of convicts; each one now bears its own honorable name,

*The table on page 27 shows the trends in United States submarines from 1900 to the latest vessels to slide down the ways.

DEVELOPMENT OF UNITED STATES SUBMARINES, 1898 TO 1942

Date	Designation	Class Name	Number	Length	Displacement (tons)		Speed (knots)		Horsepower		Torpedo Tubes	Cruising Radius (miles)	Men	Cost
					Surface	Submerged	Surface	Submerged	Surface	Submerged				
1898		Holland	1	53' 3"	about 61	73	6	5	50	75	1	200		
1899	A	Plunger	7	64'	106	122	8	7	160	70	1	490	8	$ 170,000
1904	B	Viper	3	82'	145	170	9	8	250	115	2	850	10	200,000
1906	C	Octopus	5	105'	239	274	8	8	500	230	2	850	18	250,000
1906	D	Narwhal	3	134'	288	337	13	9	600	330	4	900	18	360,000
1908	E	Skipjack	2	135' 2"	287	342	13	11	600	330	4	1,240	19	369,650
1908	F	Carp	4	142' 7"	330	400	13	11	620	620	4	4,450	21	454,740
1908	G.	Seal	4	161'	400	515	14	10	1,200	750	6	3,500	21	450,000
1909	H	Seawolf	3	150' 3"	358	434	14	10.5	950	620	4	4,450	22	491,000
1909	K	Haddock	8	153' 6"	392	521	14	10.5	950	680	4	5,500	25	469,000
1911	L		7	168' 5"	450	548	14.5	10.5	900	680	4	5,500	27	534,000
1913	L		4	165'	451	527	14	10.5	1,200	800	4	5,500	27	535,000
1913	M		1	196' 3"	488	676	14.8	9.8	840	680	4	5,500	29	615,000
1914	N		7	147' 3"	347	414	13.1	10.6	960	560	4	5,500	26	450,000
1916	T		3	269' 9"	1,106	1,484	21	11.5	4,400	1,520	6	3,000 (at 14 knots)	45	1,350,000
1916	O		16	172'	520	629	14	10	900	760	4	6,000	30	550,000
1916	R		27	186'	569	680	13.5	10.5	880	882	4	4,800	30	692,000
1916	S		41	220'	800	1,092	14.5	10	1,200	1,761	4 or 5	5,500	38	1,300,000
1916	S		10	225'	956	1,126	14.5	10	1,200	1,500	4	7,600 to 10,000	38	
1918	V	Barracuda	3	334' 6"	2,065	2,160	19	8	7,100	2,400	6	10,000+	75	
1920	V	Argonaut*	3	371'	2,730	3,960	15	8	5,450	**	6	12,000+	88	
1932	D	Dolphin	1	319'	1,540	2,215	17	8	4,200	**	6	12,000+	63	
1934	C	Cachalot	2	272'	1,120	1,650	17	8.5	1,800	**	6	12,000+	45	
1936	P	Porpoise	4	301'	1,315	1,908	20	8.5	4,500	**	6	12,000+	50	4,000,000
1937	P	Perch	6	301'	1,330	1,998	20	8.5	4,500	**	6	12,000+	50	4,000,000
1938	S	Salmon	6	308'	1,450	2,198	20	8.5	5,600	**	8	12,000+	55	5,500,000
1939	S	Sargo	6	310'	1,450	2,200	**	**	**	**	**	**	55	5,500,000
1940	S	Seadragon	4	310'	1,450	2,200	**	**	**	**	**	**	55	5,500,000
1940		Tambor	6	310'	1,475	**	**	**	**	**	**	**	**	5,500,000
1941		Mackerel	7	**		900	**	**	**	**	**	**	**	5,500,000
1941		Gar	6	**		1,500	**	**	**	**	**	**	**	5,500,000
1942		Gato	6	**		1,500	**	**	**	**	**	**	**	5,500,000

*The *Argonaut* itself has but four tubes.
**These figures are secret information and are not available.

just like all the other fighting ships. Appropriately enough, they are given the names of fish and other aquatic creatures. Cryptic letters and numbers are no more inscribed upon the superstructures. Officially, all submarines are listed by the Navy in the class designated by the letters SS, and each vessel has its own number in that class. In wartime submarines do not bear names or numbers on their bodies.

The cost of a modern submarine is now in the neighborhood of $5,500,000.

THE PARTS OF A SUBMARINE

Structurally, the modern submarine is divided into eight compartments, separated from each other by steel partitions. The only connection between them is one watertight, oval doorway barely large enough for an average-sized man to squeeze through. In case of trouble in any compartment, it can be completely sealed and segregated from all of the others.

Up in the bow of the submarine is the forward torpedo room. Far forward in this compartment is the impressive array of breech doors of the tubes from which the torpedoes are launched; in this compartment, too, are stored in side racks the reserve torpedoes, in addition to those which are carried in the tubes ready for action. The number of tubes is a bit of information which the Navy properly considers nobody's business but its own, but the modern submarine has been variously, if unofficially, reputed to have "from eight to ten," four or six in the bow and four in the stern. In this compartment is also located the highly complicated and secret listening device, which enables the submarine not only to pick up the sounds of other vessels, but even to identify their types by the noises made by their engines and to compute their speed by counting the audible beats of their propellers a minute. The beat of the propellers of a battleship, for instance, is quite unlike the light whir made by the propellers of a destroyer; even without the aid of the hydrophones the roar made by a destroyer passing overhead at the modest pace of 25 knots sounds like that of an express train. So delicate is this instrument that the sound of vessels miles away may be picked up, and so sensitive is it that even such "water noises" as air bubbles, gravel rolling on the sea bottom, the surf pounding on distant shores, and the peculiar squeaks made by schools of fish sound like static on the radio.

Just aft of the forward torpedo room is the forward battery room, so called because below its deck are kept the massive electric storage batteries that furnish motive power to the vessel when it is submerged. These batteries, each cell of which is almost as high as a man and weighs more than half a ton, cost over $100,000; in bulk they would be a load for three freight cars. Each cell generates two volts; consequently, the standard equipment of 120 cells generates a total of 240 volts; some submarines carry even more. Running at maximum submerged speed on its batteries, a submarine can go about 10 miles before the batteries must be recharged; at very low speed it can go almost 100 miles.

WHERE THE OFFICERS LIVE

The forward battery room itself (above the compartment where the batteries are stored) is "officer country." Here are the amazingly compact living quarters of the commissioned personnel, right across the passageway from the cubbyholes that boast the designation of "offices" (smaller even than telephone booths) of the noncommissioned staff. In comparison to the primitive accommodations for officers on the

An American Sub Fighting Off German Stukas

earlier submarines, these quarters are palatial—not so spacious as a Pullman compartment, of course, but more tightly packed with conveniences.

The captain's cabin, which measures 6 feet 3 inches square, is a marvel of scientific planning; besides the berth, designed for an average-sized captain, it contains a desk, a chest of drawers, a shiny steel washbowl with hot and cold running water, an electric heater, racks for clothing (all built in, of course), and such refinements as a gyrocompass dial, a depth gauge, and a couple of telephones, as well as an assortment of other instruments, all illuminated by an indirect lighting system.

The wardroom, which corresponds to the grand salon of a luxury liner, is no wider but it is a bit longer. Around its dining table eight men can be seated in a pinch, and if eight men try it, that is the way they will be seated. Its compact cupboards contain the ship's silver and linen; a five-foot bookshelf constitutes the ship's library.

Adjoining this is a pantry large enough to hold one mess attendant of medium bulk, provided he stands upright at the miniature electric cooker and electric refrigerator and keeps his elbows down. Near the captain's stateroom, in the latest types of submarines, is the radio room.

WHERE SAILORS EAT AND SLEEP

Aft of the forward battery room is the all-important control room, below the conning tower (see page 26). Immediately aft of that is what is flatteringly called the messroom; actually it is a dinette, and not a very big one at that. It is furnished with narrow tables that fold up, and with settees that are attached to the deck. As the compartment can seat only half of the crew at a time, the men eat in relays. Because of the limited opportunities for recreation aboard, Uncle Sam has considerately allotted a bigger ration allowance to the submariners on the correct assumption that by observing the ancient formula of "feeding the brute" he can keep him happy; the result is that the cuisine of a submarine is

admittedly the best in the Navy. Hot soup, sandwiches, pie, and various snacks are always to be had for the asking, and, of course, the inevitable "cuppa cawfee," ever on tap throughout the Navy. Enough provisions can be carried to last for months at a time—not unappetizing emergency rations, but real food, including even such luxuries as ice cream and strawberries. "They're good for the morale," says the mess officer.

Down the hatch, under the messroom, and extending under part of the control room, too, are ice-machines, the refrigerator rooms for keeping meats and frozen foods, the chill room for storing fresh vegetables, dry storerooms for keeping such items as canned goods, flour, and sugar, and the gun-ammunition magazines. Between meals the messroom becomes a lounging center for men off duty; for entertainment purposes they have books, magazines, and the inevitable radio. Following the jovial custom of the Navy (and Army, too, for that matter), the men have a slang name for every item of food

Crew Space Is Limited

on the menu, all of them uncomplimentary and most of them improper. Spinach alone has been spared; it is called just spinach.

The compartment aft of the messroom is known merely as the "crew space"; it is crowded mostly with tiers of metal-springed bunks. Because the compartment can accommodate only about thirty-two, other bunks are scattered about the submarine wherever space can be found—in the forward and after torpedo rooms, for instance. Within reach of each bunk is the occupant's locker, 20 by 30 inches in size, wherein he may store any worldly possessions except liquor, living creatures, or perishable articles that might become a public nuisance. Adjoining this dormitory is the washroom, which includes what are probably the most compact shower baths in the world.

Next in order comes the engine room, distinguished principally by a narrow passageway down the center flanked by compact masses of machinery. Here are the Diesel engines and electric generators, capable of developing more than 5,000 horsepower; at full speed they can drive the vessel on the surface at 20 knots or better.

In the maneuvering room, just aft, are the electric motors which drive the propeller shafts. These motors receive their source of power, electricity, from the Diesel generators when on the surface. The instant a submarine submerges, the engines are stopped, but the motors continue to turn the propellers. In that instant the electrical controls are operated to shift the load to the main storage batteries, which can drive the boat under water at a speed up to 9 or 10 knots. It is not of primary importance, however, for a submarine to attain great underwater speed; its role is to lie in wait and stalk its quarry, hastening its pace only for short distances in order to place itself in a favorable firing position or to escape danger.

Last of all comes the after torpedo room, which is pretty much a replica of the forward torpedo room and in some vessels just as important. The modern submarine carries almost as many stings in its tail as in its head, and can pack a whole series of wallops both coming and going.

The Engine Room, Source of the Sub's Motive Power

An American Sub Submerges

CHAPTER VII

The Control Room: The Brains of the Modern "Pig Boat"

IN NAVY LINGO the submarine is ordinarily known as a "pig boat," but sometimes it is less politely called a "sewer pipe," because of the slight odor that clings to the members of its crew after a sustained submergence. But that is the respectable and honorable odor of Diesel oil.

The interior of a pig boat contains a greater volume of more intricate machinery than any other class of vessel afloat. A trip through the narrow passageway—at times nothing more than a catwalk—that extends from stem to stern is suggestive of the trip of a minute insect through the compact mechanisms of a well-made watch, provided the watch were designed in the shape of a long, slim panatela cigar. Yet the basic principle upon which a submarine operates is simple enough.

HOW THE SUBMARINE DIVES

When a submarine submerges, it fills its various ballast tanks with water in order to reduce its buoyancy, and down the vessel goes. If the boat is properly trimmed, she submerges on a practically even keel, with perhaps as little as a five-degree down angle as the diving planes guide her below the surface. Ordinarily, too, when the Kingston valves are opened to admit the inflow of water ballast, the vents are opened to permit the escape of air. In case of emergency, when a rapid submergence is demanded, a "quick dive" brings the submarine to periscope depth (which in some of the earlier models was considered 40 feet, but which is now a naval secret) within 60 or 70 seconds. The quick dive used to be called a "crash dive," but that word "crash" had psychological connotations which were unpleasant and the word was eliminated. When a quick dive is about to be made, the skipper gives the command "Ride the vents," which means that the flood valves are opened but the vents are kept closed to offset the sudden increase in water pressure. The largest of our submarines take in as much as 1,230 tons of water to put them in readiness for a dive.

THE DEPTH GAUGES

Both air and water manifolds are operated from the control room, located amidships, which is the post of the commanding officer. (The commanding officer of a submarine is formally addressed as "Captain," informally as "Skipper," but his official rank is usually lieutenant or lieutenant commander.) This control room is the brain and nerve center of the submarine: in it all decisions are made; from it all orders emanate. Here is the center of the submarine communication system; if anything happens to this compartment, all communication between the other compartments is cut off. Here are located the depth gauges, "the most important instruments" on a pig boat, which register the depth of the submarine. It is naturally of the utmost importance always to know precisely how far under the surface—and how far above the sea bottom—the vessel is navigating. Should it be insufficiently submerged, the periscope or conning tower would show and thus reveal its presence; should it be down too deep, the vessel would be endangered by the water pressure. All submarines are designed to withstand the pressure at 200 feet, but most of the new ones are built to go down safely to 300 feet at least. Should it sink to really great depths, the boat would crumple like an eggshell. That is why the dials of the depth gauges are under constant surveillance.

Checking the Depth Gauges

32

Here in the control room, too, is the aneroid barometer, which indicates the air pressure within the boat itself. This is a negligible amount of pressure—just enough to make sure that the boat is really watertight and that no air is escaping through some small but potentially dangerous leak. Here is the "supersonical" fathometer, which by means of reflected sound waves indicates the distance between the submarine and the sea bottom. Here are the controls of the stern and bow planes, which guide the course of a submarine under water somewhat as the horizontal rudders of an airplane guide its course through the air. Here is the master gyroscope, as well as the little instrument known as the "clinometer," which tells the degree of the list of the vessel. Indeed, the entire control room is such a compact mass of glistening valves, levers, throttles, clutches, pushbuttons, and all manner of gadgets that there is no space for anyone except the members of the crew at their stations. The most gay and festive of the mechanical doodads is the indicator box, which is illuminated by rows of green and red signal lights that reveal just what hull and tank valves are open or shut; it is appropriately known as "the Christmas tree."

THE EYE OF THE PIG BOAT

But the focal point in the control room is the periscope. When the submarine is submerged, the periscope is its eye; here is the post of the commanding officer. What the skipper sees—and does not see—serves as the basis for his decisions and for his actions. At the command "Up periscope!" the shiny steel cylinder is shot upward by electrically operated hoists, and the captain takes his place at the eyepiece, clutching the horizontal handles that control the movement of the lenses above. In time of action, it is a moment full of tension. A hush falls over the compartment as all eyes are turned toward the captain, seeking to interpret from his actions and from the expression on his face the significance of what he sees. Before him, with his hands upon the steering wheel, stands the quartermaster; toward his rear stands the navigator, poring over his charts, spread upon a narrow built-in desk. Within reach of his arm is a battery of pushbuttons for signaling instructions throughout the ship. All the captain's orders are given quietly, almost in an undertone. The tension relaxes only when the periscope is ordered down.

It is a far cry from the early days when a submarine had to "porpoise" in order to catch a fleeting glimpse of the surface through the ports of the primitive conning tower. Even the periscopes of some of the earlier models of Uncle Sam's underwater craft were little more than modified camera obscuras, which gave only a shadowy reflection of the scene above.

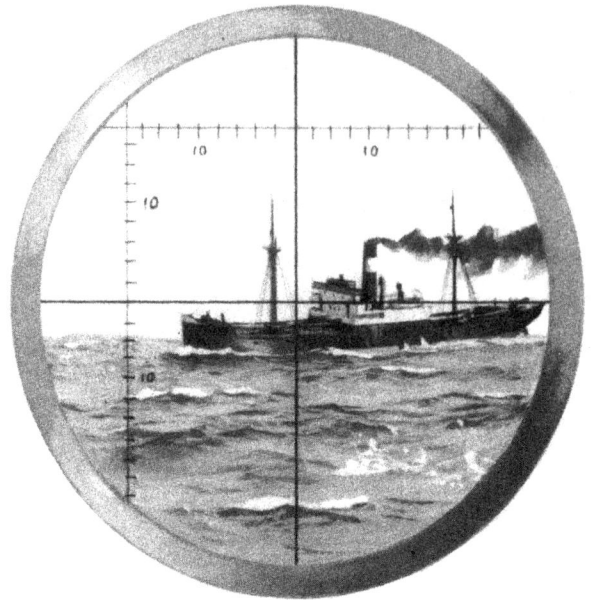
The Victim Is Spotted

The Skipper Takes His Post at the Periscope

The modern periscope is a precision instrument built with a double tube. The inside tube, which contains the optical system, is filled with nitrogen under a pressure of about 5 pounds to the square inch, which keeps the vision clear of mist. The lenses are equipped with ray filters, to increase visibility under varying atmospheric conditions. The modern periscopes, too, are fitted with range-finders and with high and low magnification adjustments. They are of three kinds. One is called the "altiscope," which gives a zenith view used for searching the skies for aircraft; one is the "night periscope," with a high efficiency in light transmission; and the third is the "attack periscope," with a small head which is as inconspicuous as possible. And the modern submarine is furnished with two of each—"just in case."

THE PIG BOAT'S VOICE AND EARS

The radio shack is tucked away in a cubbyhole of its own either in or adjacent to the control room. It is packed with long-range radio sets, but just what they are and how they operate and how far they can reach are details around which a veil of official secrecy is tightly drawn. It is no secret that the electromagnetic oscillator devices, built into the hulls for underwater signaling, have a transmitting range up to about 50 miles, while the hydrophones, using the K-tube, have an acoustic radius ranging up to about three miles. Because of the intensity of their sounds, the oscillator and an exploding depth charge can be heard at a much greater distance than a propeller.

And just as on the big ships of the Navy, the radiomen are all called "Sparks."

A SHIP THAT NEVER REACHED PORT

The gun crew of a Nazi submarine keeps firing as the survivors of a torpedoed Allied cargo ship put off in lifeboats. The officers watch with grim satisfaction as another Allied "shipping bottom" with a badly-needed cargo founders. They chalk up another victim for the Axis submarine campaign; but they also are subject to sudden death.

Subs alongside a Submarine Tender

CHAPTER VIII

Air for the Submariners

IN NORMAL TIMES a submarine navigates under water only for brief periods: long enough to make routine practice dives, engage in torpedo practice, and participate in maneuvers. In wartime, however, the submarine keeps submerged most of the time after she leaves her base; for remaining on the surface during daylight hours would invite attack, particularly by enemy submarines and planes. Consequently the wartime procedure is to surface only at night, both to get a supply of fresh air and to start the Diesel engines going in order to recharge the electric storage batteries. Thus the problem of ventilation is ordinarily a simple one; only after a submergence of several hours does the submariner become conscious of stale air, battery emanations, and the smell of cooking, none of which bother him as much as the fact that he cannot keep his cigarette burning.

BREATHING UNDER WATER

When the boat first submerges, she carries down with her a supply of fresh air which is kept in constant circulation throughout all of the compartments by means of motors. This is enough to keep the crew comfortably supplied with air for as long as twenty-four hours, should that ever become necessary. If an emergency demands longer submergence, the "bad air," technically known as carbon dioxide, or CO_2, and harmless in concentrations up to 3 per cent, may begin to cause trouble. The men begin to breathe more deeply, to move with greater effort, to make errors in judgment. When that point is reached, the air purification system is put into effect. This consists of spreading about a white powder which is popularly known as soda lime but which is in reality a secret chemical referred to merely as a "CO_2 absorbent." When the carbon dioxide concentration reaches 4 per cent, distress in breathing and in moving is definitely increased; a man may faint from exhaustion caused by just raising his arm. At 5 per cent the distress becomes acute. In extreme cases, when men are awaiting rescue, for example, oxygen may be released from the tanks reserved for filling up the escape lungs (described on page 46). Fifty hours is about the

35

present practical limit for continued submergence. The record for continuous submergence was made on a test by the United States submarine *O-10,* which remained under water for ninety-six hours (four full days) with a crew of thirty-three men aboard; during the entire time the amount of carbon dioxide never exceeded 2.4 per cent.

Another hazard, which has been so carefully guarded against that accidents due to it in the United States Navy are negligible, is hydrogen gas. This is the ordinary, highly inflammable gas used for inflating balloons. It is created—if it is created at all—while the batteries are being charged. Because it can be neither smelled nor seen, an automatic detector machine is used to record its presence. A mixture of 4 per cent is considered highly inflammable; 8 per cent is so explosive that a spark from a pipe would almost certainly set it off.

On rare occasions, when salt water comes into contact with the electric storage batteries, the deadly chlorine gas is created. This is a heavy, greenish-yellow gas with an unmistakable, pungent odor, and is easily detected by both the nose and the eye. As soon as this is discovered, the alarm is sounded, the compartment in which it is discovered is vacated and the emergency doors are closed, the crew don their Momsen lungs as gas masks, and the vessel surfaces with all speed.

ANOTHER KIND OF AIR

One form of gas is noticeably less prevalent in a submarine than in any other type of Navy vessel; it is colloquially known as "hot air." Submariners are a strangely silent crew when at their diving stations. One reason is that each man is at his post of duty throughout the ship, and each post is important. Another is that every command must be heard and must be obeyed; the failure of a single man to hear and to execute an order may place the entire crew in peril. That is why such a subdued air prevails during navigation under water. Only the quiet voice of the captain is heard, and the voices of subordinates who transmit his commands.

Flooding the Ballast Tanks

36

CHAPTER IX

Battle Stations in the Torpedo Room

The Prime Weapon of the Submarine: The Torpedo

IN THE control room the men are on the alert at their battle stations. The captain is at his post at the periscope. The silence is broken by the command:

"Make ready Number One torpedo tube."

The order is instantly transmitted to the forward torpedo room, where the torpedomen are busy—opening valves, building up air pressure, checking firing circuits and ready lights.

"Number One tube ready," comes the reply from the torpedo room.

The top-ranking enlisted man on board, known as the "Chief of the Boat," stands in the control room with his hand on the firing circuit, his eyes riveted on the ready lights.

"All ready, sir," he reports.

Throughout the boat all is quiet; only the low, distant hum of the electric motors is heard.

"Stand by!"

A moment of tension follows; all eyes in the control room are fixed on the captain's face at the periscope. The bow planesman anticipates the next command by moving the bow planes

to hard dive, in order to prevent the bow of the vessel from being forced upward when the torpedo leaves its tube.

"Fire!"

Thud! A gentle quiver runs through the boat.

The Number One torpedo is projected on its underwater course with much the same sort of dull sound, on a magnified scale, as is made by the familiar cash carrier in the department store when it is inserted into the pneumatic tube system. The torpedoman instantly jerks up the vent to let the sea water into the tube left vacant by the torpedo; the act must be performed quickly or the buoyancy of the boat will be affected, and the boat will tend to rise at the bow—a movement that in battle might well betray the submarine's location. The torpedo is "fired," or, more properly, launched, on the same principle as the cash carrier—by compressed air. As a matter of precaution, the door at the breech of the torpedo tube is so interlocked with the door at the muzzle that only one can be opened at a time. Lack of this mechanism has caused at least two

37

great submarine disasters; in both cases the inner door was opened without realization that the muzzle door was open and the tube was therefore full of water and open to the sea.

From the moment a torpedo is launched it proceeds on its way under its own motive power. This is furnished by a flask containing air at a pressure of 2,000 pounds or more to the square inch; this "air-flask" constitutes the central part of the torpedo. The longer the air-flask is, the greater is the running range of the torpedo; the greater the speed at which the torpedo is adjusted to run, the more energy it consumes and consequently the shorter the distance it can travel. When it is adjusted to speed along at a 40-knot clip or better, it may cover a distance of —well, that is a Navy secret. But it is no secret that in peacetime practice the range extends up to 10,000 yards, or about five miles.

THE PARTS OF A TORPEDO

That part of the torpedo which is in front of the air-flask is the "war head." In peacetime practice these war heads are nonexplosive; when the torpedoes have run their course, they float about until they are retrieved to be used again. In wartime the torpedoes are fitted with war heads containing T.N.T., together with the devices that explode the charges when they hit the target. Unless they hit the target, they run along until the power is exhausted; then they sink.

The third important part of the torpedo is in the rear; it is called the "afterbody." This contains the engine as well as the depth and steering controls, all of them items of a secret nature and all of them expensive. The depth engine, which regulates the distance below the surface at which the torpedo is set to travel, is operated by hydrostatic pressure, which increases .44 of a pound for each foot of submergence; this in turn operates the horizontal rudders that keep the torpedo at the determined depth. A spinning gyroscope controls the devices operating the vertical rudder that keeps the torpedo on its course.

With its shiny steel body, its pointed nose, and its tapering stern furnished with two tiny propellers, the torpedo looks enough like a "fish" to justify the nickname that has been applied to it. The present-day torpedo ranges up to 20 feet in length, weighs 2,500 or more pounds, and is of a standard diameter of 21 inches; the smaller torpedoes (used in the older and smaller submarines) have a standard diameter of 18 inches.

"AIMING" THE FISH

Contrary to common belief, torpedoes are not aimed by those who man them; their job is to see that the machinery is in perfect trim, and to load and discharge the torpedoes upon command. The torpedoes are "aimed" only to the extent that the vessel itself is aimed. The trick is to discharge a torpedo, set to travel at a known speed, on a selected firing course and at a specified depth, from a submarine proceeding at a known speed, at just the precise moment that will make the missile come into contact with a target moving at an estimated speed in an estimated direction and at an estimated distance. And that requires a bit of figuring which only the man at the periscope is in a position to do.

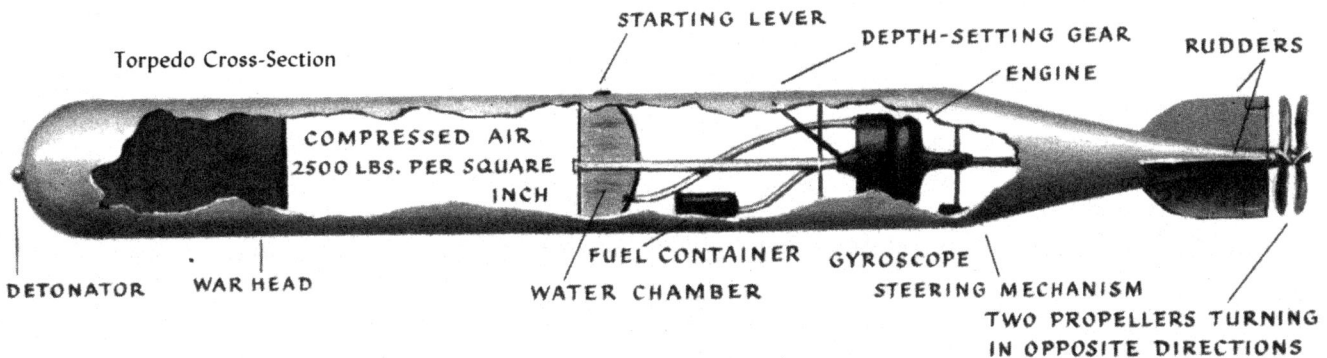

Torpedo Cross-Section

STARTING LEVER

DEPTH-SETTING GEAR

RUDDERS

ENGINE

COMPRESSED AIR 2500 LBS. PER SQUARE INCH

DETONATOR

WAR HEAD

FUEL CONTAINER

WATER CHAMBER

GYROSCOPE

STEERING MECHANISM

TWO PROPELLERS TURNING IN OPPOSITE DIRECTIONS

Saving Human Lives — Survivors of the *Squalus* Disaster Are Rescued

CHAPTER X

Submarine Rescue Ships and Rescue Chambers

O NE CLASS of vessel in Uncle Sam's Navy has no counterpart anywhere in the world. It is the submarine rescue ship. The development of this rescue ship, together with its now famous "rescue chamber," is in line with the Navy's dictum that it is more important to save men than to save materiel. Significantly enough, it came as the direct result of the sinking of the submarine *S-4* off Provincetown, Massachusetts, on December 17, 1927, with a loss of forty lives. After that tragedy a board of naval officers and civilians was convened by the Secretary of the Navy; a few months later that board came out of its huddle with an idea.

Briefly, it was an idea for a modified form of diving bell that could be lowered by cable and attached to the escape hatch of the sunken submarine, making it possible to open the hatch, transfer the men to the rescue chamber, and then hoist them to the surface. It was facetiously called the "undersea elevator." So sound did

this idea strike the Navy that it invested in five rescue ships with full equipment. Then year after year passed, happily without an emergency call; during all that period the rescue vessels were held in readiness. Twice a year practice cruises were made in collaboration with submarines, and men were "rescued" from vessels resting on the bottom. Experimental work was carried on, crews were trained to locate sunken submarines, money was being spent, divers and salvage workers were kept on the alert. Foreign navies expressed no interest at all in these proceedings further than a tolerant amusement over this new example of a "Yankee notion." In the meantime, submarines of other navies would occasionally sink, and when they did their crews were drowned; it was considered one of the hazards inherent in the submarine service. True, there have been occasions when men have miraculously escaped in an air bubble rumbling out of a hatch after the compartment has been flooded nearly full, and escapes via the torpedo tubes have been recorded, but these are as rare as fleas on an iron dog.

THE FIRST TEST

Then in a flash the chance for demonstration came. On May 23, 1939, the country was shocked with the report of the sinking of the *Squalus* in 240 feet of water off Portsmouth, New Hampshire. Messages from the trapped victims revealed that thirty-three men of the crew of fifty-nine were still alive. The rescue ship *Falcon*, which for years had been held in readiness at New London, Connecticut, for just such an emergency, was off to the scene in almost a matter of minutes. Then it was that the public learned that such a thing as a submarine rescue ship even existed; it was electrified a few hours later to discover not only that there was such a device as a rescue chamber but that it really worked. The country held its breath as it listened to radio reports of the proceedings.

Every one of the thirty-three trapped survivors was saved. After a decade of waiting and preparation, the rescue ship "experiment" was vindicated. Today Uncle Sam has eleven rescue ships, built and building.

THE RESCUE CHAMBER

The rescue chamber is a steel structure that weighs about nine tons. Ovoid in shape, it is ten feet high, about nine feet in diameter at the top, and tapers off to about five feet in diameter across the bottom, which is flat, giving it somewhat the appearance of the egg reputedly set upright on its end by Columbus. Inside, the chamber is divided into an upper compartment, which contains most of the operating gear and in which the passengers ride, and a lower compartment which is open to the sea at the bottom. This lower compartment is connected with the upper compartment by a standard watertight hatch. The upper chamber is furnished with fourteen portable tanks, each with a capacity of

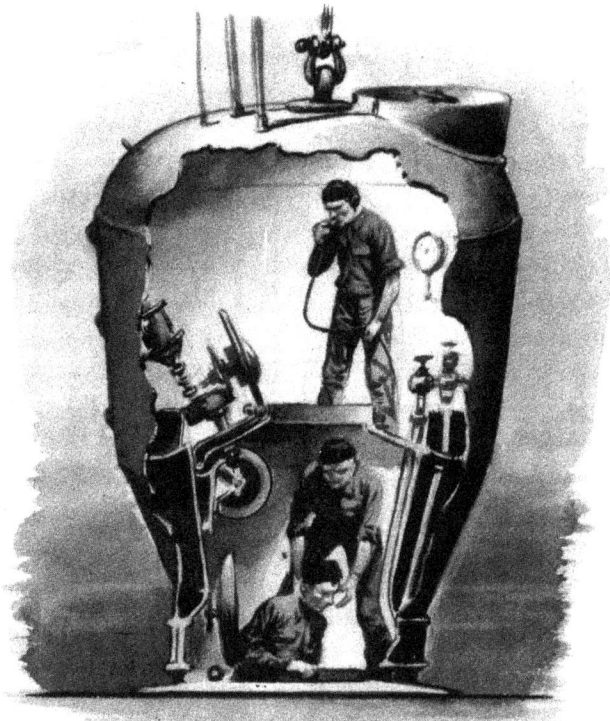

The Rescue Chamber in Operation

sixty-seven pounds of salt water, which may be filled or emptied as needed to compensate for the entrances and exits of passengers. The lower compartment is completely surrounded by a ballast tank. When in use, the rescue chamber is adjusted so that it has 1,000 pounds of positive buoyancy. That means a pull of 1,000 pounds or more is required to get it under the water.

HOW IT WORKS

Stripped of technical details, this is the way the rescue chamber works:

The rescue ship anchors near the sunken submarine, lays out a mooring directly over it, and brings the rescue chamber alongside. Then it makes all the connections between the chamber and the rescue ship—electric power lines, compressed-air lines, and the telephone wires. Next, a diver is sent down, taking with him the "downhaul" cable, which he attaches to the spindle of the submarine's escape hatch. Thus a direct contact is made between the sunken submarine and the rescue chamber.

40

Next, the rescue chamber's crew of two men enter the upper compartment, flood the lower compartment, and turn on the air motor that reels the chamber downward on the down-haul cable and lands it directly over the victim's escape hatch. The rubber-gasketed bottom of the rescue chamber fits over the seat of the escape hatch, which was built for just this purpose. Then the water in the lower compartment of the rescue chamber is blown out by compressed air; as this is done, the pressure of the sea against the top of the chamber naturally holds it as tight as a blister against the submarine's skin. Now it is safe to open the hatch between the upper and lower compartments; through this one of the operators descends and secures the rescue chamber to the submarine by means of four holding-down lugs, also provided for just this purpose. Now the escape hatch of the submarine can be opened, and through it the entrapped men can ascend first into the lower and then into the upper compartment of the rescue chamber. The space is large enough to hold six men at a time, but a dozen may be squeezed into it if necessary. The rescue chamber that saved the thirty-three members of the crew of the *Squalus* made four trips.

Now all that remains to be done is to transport the rescued men from the submarine to the rescue ship on the surface by means of this "underseas elevator." The upward journey begins by resealing the escape hatch of the submarine, flooding the lower compartment of the rescue chamber (which breaks the vacuum seal that holds it against the submarine), and blowing enough water from the portable tanks to compensate for the weight of the passengers. As soon as the ballast tank is blown, the rescue chamber rises by its own buoyancy—held in check by the unwinding reel with the motor in reverse.

THIRTY-THREE FATHOMS DOWN

The depth at which such rescues may be effected depends entirely upon the capacity of the diver who carries down the down-haul cable to withstand the high pressure of the deep water. A second-class diver in the Navy gets his rating by operating at 90 feet; to win the rate of first-class diver he must operate at 200-foot depths. A few of the experts can go to even greater depths for short intervals and still maintain their faculties sufficiently to perform their duties. During recent years the use of helium gas mixed with the oxygen pumped down to them has greatly increased the efficiency of the divers. When subjected to a pressure of 100 pounds to the square inch, a diver gets lightheaded and his actions become slow and erratic; he becomes intoxicated in much the same way as a man gets drunk on liquor. Few men above thirty-five can "take it."

The unique advantage of the rescue chamber over all other like devices lies in the fact that it permits the escape of the men without submitting them to high pressure and without requiring them to flood the submarine compartment and escape through the water. There is no air pressure in the chamber and there is none in the submarine; consequently there is no danger of the dreaded "bends." The men do not even get wet.

Some day, before the long-advertised but indefinitely postponed millennium arrives, perhaps the navies of the world will co-operate in the name of humanity to the extent of standardizing the escape hatches of their submarines so that rescue chambers can be adjusted to them all. Today, only Uncle Sam's submarines are built to fit the rescue chambers, and only American submarines can benefit from the "Yankee notion." At about the same time as the *Squalus* sank, the English submarine *Thetis,* the French submarine *Phénix,* and the Japanese submarine *I-63* met with similar but more tragic disasters, with the loss of practically all aboard. Even had an American rescue vessel been at the scene of each disaster, it would have been unable to render aid. The hatches of the foreign vessels were not built to permit the adjustment of the American rescue chamber — and they had no rescue chambers of their own.

Sub against Sub

CHAPTER XI

Some Facts to Remember about Submarines

THE THREE standard sound signals, all audible throughout the submarine, are produced by the klaxon (the final warning before diving), the siren (the collision alarm), and the bells (the general alarm).

⚓ ⚓ ⚓

Smoke bombs, for use as signals from submerged submarines, are released from the "underwater signal ejector." The water melts a thin wafer in the shell, and the chemical action of the water causes an explosion that sends a bomb 175 feet into the air. (A red bomb is a call for help; a yellow bomb is released three minutes before a submarine surfaces during maneuvers, as a warning to vessels above; and black, white, and green bombs are used as signals during tactical exercises.) ⚓ ⚓ ⚓

When a submarine becomes disabled under water and cannot surface, it releases marker buoys on which is inscribed "Submarine — sunk here. Telephone inside."

⚓ ⚓ ⚓

Momsen escape lungs are located in each end compartment, one for each man in the crew.

Emergency food lockers located in every compartment, for use only in case of accident, contain a can of baked beans, a spoon, a couple of candles, and a flashlight, for each man. (Unless rescue comes, this will supply a man with food for the rest of his life.)

⚓ ⚓ ⚓

Each living compartment of a modern submarine has connections to which "soup lines" may be attached by divers, so that, pending rescue, fresh air and liquid food may be furnished to men trapped in a disabled vessel.

⚓ ⚓ ⚓

No alcoholic drinks are permitted aboard a submarine—or any other Navy vessel. (Violators face such stiff penalties as demotion, a bad-conduct discharge, six months in the hoosegow, or fine of a half year's pay.)

⚓ ⚓ ⚓

Only when "the smoking lamp is lit," meaning when the captain passes the word, are the men of a submarine permitted to use tobacco. In the days of sailing ships a lamp was actually provided; today only the picturesque phrase is retained.

A submarine does not carry a ship's doctor, nor has it room for a sick bay (the Navy's term for "infirmary"). Submariners must either keep well or be dosed by the pharmacist's mate, whose drugs and equipment come out of the medical locker.　♒　♒　♒

There are usually five ways to enter a submarine. Each is through a standard hatchway, 23 inches in diameter, on the top deck. One leads down into the forward torpedo room, one into the crew's space, one into the engine room, one into the control room, and one into the after torpedo room. Most of these same openings also serve as escape hatches.

　　　　♒　♒　♒

A submarine may be steered either from the control room or from the conning tower. Electric or hydraulic power is used, with hand power always available in case of need.

　　　　♒　♒　♒

So seaworthy are submarines that they can outride the stoutest gales; none has ever been known to capsize. In violent hurricanes a submarine *could* submerge and proceed serenely below the surface, but as this consumes battery power, it is not an approved procedure.

　　　　♒　♒　♒

While submerged, a submarine must keep moving (unless on the sea floor) or it will get out of control. It cannot hover in the water any better than an airplane can hover in the sky.

　　　　♒　♒　♒

The underwater movements of a submarine are guided by its diving planes—ponderous, flapperlike wings at the bow and stern that are extended like fins only when the craft is submerging.　♒　♒　♒

Resting on the bottom, or "bottoming," is a common practice of submarines when in shoal water; to rise they simply blow their tanks and "slide off." By cutting off their various motors and pumps they can lie in hiding from listening enemies and at the same time save fuel.

Compressed air for blowing the ballast tanks is carried in steel flasks at a pressure of about 2,500 pounds to the square inch; special "impulse flasks" are employed for discharging the torpedoes, and flasks containing air at a pressure of 1,200 pounds to the square inch are used for starting the Diesel engines. The compressed air is sometimes released into the boat to freshen the atmosphere.　♒　♒　♒

The Diesel engine, the invention of Otto Diesel, a German, was first used in a submarine in 1912. It has been aptly said that "the modern submarine owes its existence to the Diesel engine, the storage battery, and the tin can."

　　　　♒　♒　♒

A submarine has two telephone systems. One is the regular interdepartmental service telephone, and the other is the "battle station" telephone system, for use only when the crew is set for action.　♒　♒　♒

To keep a submarine "in trim"—or balanced —every pound of weight must be computed, including the number of men aboard and the supplies carried; even the fuel consumed and the waste ejected must be compensated for. The trim is disturbed even by the passage of the vessel from sea water into fresher water, such as at river mouths, and vice versa, owing to the differences in specific gravity. (In the good old days the trim was maintained by the primitive method of having the men run back and forth.)

　　　　♒　♒　♒

The first submarine "uniforms" consisted of any old oily clothes at all—stylishly topped off with derby hats.　♒　♒　♒

Navy officers get a bonus of 25 per cent of their base pay as long as they are on submarine duty.

　　　　♒　♒　♒

Qualified submariners, both officers and men, must pass rigid examinations before they are awarded their insignia. The insigne shows a conning tower, a bow, and bow planes, flanked by a dolphin on each side. (An officer wears a gold bar on his breast; an enlisted man wears it embroidered on his sleeve.)

Submarine Students in the Model Navigation Room

CHAPTER XII

The Making of a Submariner

THEIR WANT OF PRACTICE WILL MAKE THEM UNSKILLFUL, AND THEIR
WANT OF SKILL, TIMID. MARITIME SKILL, LIKE SKILL OF OTHER KINDS,
IS NOT TO BE CULTIVATED BY THE WAY OR AT CHANCE TIMES.
                                    —Thucydides (about 450 B.C.)

Inscription over the doorway of the Submarine School, United States Naval Base, New London, Connecticut

THE AMERICAN submariner is probably the most hand-picked sailor in the whole United States Navy. In the first place, no man gets into the submarine service unless he asks for it. In peacetime an officer cannot even ask for it until he has had two years of Navy service and made a record that will bear scrutiny; in wartime, the restrictions upon enlisted men are relaxed, and sometimes they go into the submarine service—at their own request—direct from the training station. Then the submarine service looks over the applicants and picks out those whose special qualifications are outstanding. Physically the candidate must be superior to the standards set for the general service: because of the nature of his work, he must have

practically perfect lungs, respiratory tract, and stomach; he must be free from sinus trouble and his ears must be able to withstand a pressure of 50 pounds to the square inch, because that is the minimum pressure to which he is likely to be subjected when he uses the escape lung. He is tested for his binaural sense (using both ears), needed for operating the delicate listening devices for locating sounds. He must have an even temperament, and of course he must have a clean bill of health on all nervous disorders; for peculiar mannerisms, little nervous habits, trifling though they be, get into the hair of a man's associates—all of whom are very intimate associates indeed within the compact confines of a submarine. Even the unfortunate chaps who are

44

embarrassed by the social afflictions politely known as "B.O." and halitosis are out of luck.

MEN WANTED

So the submariner is probably the most balanced, the most imperturbable, and the most dependable sailor in the Navy today, and the cream of the crop are the chief petty officers. Does not Uncle Sam recognize the superiority of the submariner by giving him from $10 to $30 a month better pay? Each man knows that his life is in the hands of any member of the crew; that is why he accepts as shipmates only those upon whom he can place reliance, whose personalities he finds congenial, whose competence is beyond question. Because these are the factors, the morale of the submarine service is reputedly the highest in the Navy. Ask any submarine man and he will tell you so. And to prove it he will cite the case of the thirty-three survivors of the submarine *Squalus*. Upon being rescued, every man chose to remain with submarines.

"Once a submariner, always a submariner" is not an empty phrase.

LIFE SAVING PRACTICE— THE LUNG TRAINING TANK

After a submariner has been tentatively accepted, he is given a test in what is known as the "lung training tank," in which he is taught how to use the submarine escape lung. (One such tank is located at New London, Connecticut, and the other is at Pearl Harbor, Hawaii.) This tank, or tower, is cylindrical in form and has the general appearance of a huge silo reaching 138 feet up into the air. Within it is a tube of fresh chlorinated water 100 feet deep; around the top of this cylinder of water runs a platform from which the trainees get their preliminary instruction and onto which they eventually emerge from the depths. Every man in the submarine service, from admiral to colored messboy, must "come up the tank" to qualify, and he must do it once a year in order to remain in the submarine service.

The Lung Training Tank and Diving Bell in Operation

To the uninitiated, the experience of coming up the tank is a bit terrifying; it rates somewhere between a death-defying aquatic act at a Coney Island carnival and a third-degree attempt at suicide. If each movement is made in strict accordance with the rules, the underwater journey will be completed without danger or discomfort. But if the candidate is of an experimental turn of mind, or if he becomes careless, he automatically disqualifies himself as a submariner and becomes the object of attention from the medical officers if not the undertaker.

THE COMPRESSION CHAMBER

The first ordeal takes place in what is technically known as the compression chamber, but which is popularly known as the "torture chamber." This is a cylindrical affair only 18 feet long and 6 feet in diameter, but into it may be packed fifteen men and two instructors. When the massive doors are closed and dogged, the air pressure is turned on. Now the air pressure at sea level is 14.7 pounds to the square inch, but within the compression chamber that is raised in about 15 minutes to 50 pounds. Ninety-four men out of a hundred can take this in their stride, but if a man has trouble with his ears or with his sinuses, or if he has an improperly fitted crown on a bad tooth or an abscess, the pressure will cause him such intense pain that he is removed not only from the chamber but in all likelihood (in case he cannot qualify later) from submarine candidacy. The pressure is so great as to force ink out of fountain pens, to shatter tightly closed watches into crumbs, and even to crumple up a sealed milk can. After the required pressure has been attained, it is reduced gradually in accordance with scientifically computed Haldane charts, in order to avoid the dreaded bends, or "compressed-air illness."

THE ESCAPE LUNG

Then the escape lungs are passed around. The lung is made of rubber and stockinet and en-closes a canister of soda lime, which absorbs the carbon dioxide generated by breathing. It looks something like a large hot-water bag, equipped with a rubber lug which the wearer holds in his teeth and through which he breathes, and a clamp that holds his nostrils closed. It is held against the chest by cords attached to the neck and waist.

This is the device that makes it possible for men to escape from a sunken submarine after it has been disabled beyond all hope of surfacing under its own power, and after the escape compartments, as a last resort, have been flooded to cause air pockets to form. In these air pockets life can be sustained for only a short period—barely long enough for trapped men to don their lungs and go one at a time up through the opened escape hatch. This means that the lung must be filled from the oxygen tanks within the air pocket, where the pressure of the air must be as great as the pressure of the water outside. As the pressure of the water (and consequently of the air) increases at the rate of .445 pounds for each foot of submergence, the 50-pound pressure applied in the compression chamber is roughly equivalent to that in the air pocket of a submarine sunk 100 feet. Any sailor who is physically unable to meet this air-compression requirement is disqualified from the submarine service because he would be unable to make an emergency escape and his life would be forfeit. Contrary to common belief, men are *not* shot out of torpedo tubes in the submarine service any more than men are shot out of cannons in the Army. These are acts performed only in the circus.

From the compression chamber the men proceed to the top of the training tower, where they become accustomed to the use of the lung by easy stages. They back down into the tank on vertical ladders until their heads are a foot or so below the surface; sure enough, they can actually breathe under water! Then they are taken down 12 feet in the small diving bell, from which they make their first experimental escapes—holding themselves back by means of the "descent line" made fast below. The standard rate of travel up that 12 feet of line is very, very slow; three minutes, to be exact. Sudden ascents from great depths may, because of the unduly rapid expansion of the air, cause the lungs of the victim to explode.

When the technique has been acquired, escapes are made from the lock 18 feet below the surface. This is a chamber built into the outer wall of the tank, with an escape hatch that opens directly into the tank. When the men are locked into this chamber, the flood valve is opened to admit water through the floor. When the water rises above the hatch that opens into the tank, an air pocket is formed in which the air pressure equalizes the water pressure outside, and the door can be opened. Through it, one by one, the men emerge, gingerly fingering their way up the descent line with the calm, deliberate movements of a slow-motion film. Every submariner must make this trip.

More perilous ascents from lower depths are offered to those who volunteer; about 80 per cent of the submariners do. The escape from the 50-foot lock is the same as from the 18-foot lock, but the escape from the 100-foot lock at the bottom is the real thing. In the first place, it is built like the escape compartment of a submarine, and the procedure of making an emergency escape from it is the same as from a submarine sunk in 100 feet of water. Once the escape procedure has been started and the compartment has been flooded, there is no turning back. Up the sailorman must go through the 23-inch escape hatch overhead—dodging under the water that covers the bottom of the "skirt" which seals the air pocket in order to make his exit and grab the ascent line. Thirty-two minutes is the maximum time that a man can be exposed to this high pressure without serious danger; the last man had better be on his way upward within that period —or else. That last man is always the experienced officer who is in charge of the group.

The candidate who completes the prelimi-nary stage of the qualifying test is ready to start his training as a submariner.

From the China Station (which in Navy lingo means anywhere in the Far East) comes the tale of a toughened skipper of a submarine who blurted out the nonorthodox command to his quartermaster: "Right the —— ——— rudder!"

"Right the —— ——— rudder, sir," dutifully responded the quartermaster. When he had put the wheel over he reported:

"The —— ——— rudder is right, sir!"

The quartermaster was exactly correct in his choice of words. Following his training, he had repeated his orders precisely as they were given; it is a practice that reduces to a minimum the likelihood of misunderstanding and accident. "There is no such thing as a minor accident on a submarine" has become almost an adage.

The submariner gets his first taste of this meticulous accuracy in the Submarine School. Because this school gives advanced training for particular duty assignments to enlisted men in special subjects not normally a part of shipboard instruction, it ranks in the Navy as a Class C school.

The basic course, which all submariners must take, deals with such subjects as the construction of a submarine and its methods of operation. By means of colored charts, models, practical talks, and wall diagrams augmented by actual instruments, the student is familiarized with the water and air manifolds, the drainage, ventilation, and salvage systems, the arrangement of the ballast and fuel tanks, and the operation of the flood valves. The most complicated and elaborate of the training devices is a reproduction of the diving-control equipment of a submarine, replete with gauges, dials, and all, on a platform which simulates the movements of a boat. From an operation board in the rear the instructor can regulate the varying conditions the submarine meets—he may suddenly change the trim, for

A TIN FISH FINDS ITS MARK

A United States submarine rises to periscope depth near a Japanese merchantman
lumbering along in a convoy. In the distance is one of the destroyers assigned to
protect these bigger, slower ships; but the U.S. submariners are too swift for even the
destroyer. Already they have launched a deadly torpedo, which has landed a direct hit.

instance—and the students must make the compensating adjustments on the instruments. The training device does for the submariner about what the Link trainer does for the aviation cadet.

But the basic course is only the beginning. There is the battery course, for example, open to electricians' mates who complete the basic course; here they study the design, construction, operation, and maintenance of the huge storage batteries upon which the submarine runs when it is submerged. There is the gyro course, open to electricians' mates who complete the battery course, where the theory, care, operation, and maintenance of the gyro are taught, together with the submarine's interior communication system. There is the Diesel-engine course, open to all engineering ratings as well as to a selected group of enlisted men, where the students learn about constructional features, maintenance, and repair of the engines which furnish the motive power to the underwater craft when they are on the surface. And there is the radio course. So, by the time a man has been graduated from these courses he has acquired a technical education that is not only essential to the Navy but places a premium upon his services to private industry. Many industrial plants, especially Diesel-powered plants and those engaged in shipbuilding, are generously sprinkled with retired submariners.

THE SUBMARINER GOES TO SEA

Not all of the basic training is confined to schoolroom work. Every few days the students are taken on submarine trips where, under the watchful eyes of their instructors, they make practical application of their book and laboratory work. Here the men learn how to operate a submarine by actually operating it, from the manipulation of a valve to the firing of a torpedo. Normally, a student makes a few dozen short dives in the course of his basic training; during that time he is introduced to the fifteen different stations and to the hundred important valves employed in a submergence. Each vessel, before it leaves port, is assigned to a special diving area of its own, as a matter of precaution. Before a dive is made, each submarine reports by radio its location, the course it proposes to steer, and the expected duration of the submergence. As soon as it comes up, it reports "Surfaced." If a vessel fails to report within thirty minutes of the time specified, the Navy unleashes all the rescue forces at its command—near-by ships, airplanes, and the nearest available rescue ship, with its rescue chamber and complement of divers.

Such extraordinary safety measures are taken throughout the entire submarine service, however, that accidents are extremely rare. Despite the admitted hazards of duty with the undersea craft, statistics show that the mortality rate from all causes in the submarine service is only 3.60 per 1,000 as compared to 1.53 in the Navy as a whole. This means a difference of only about two fatalities per thousand — a variation so slight that it has failed to have any effect upon insurance rates or to arouse any trace of superstition among the submariners themselves, who are a levelheaded and untemperamental lot. Their faith in each other, in their officers, and in their boat cannot be shaken by any hoodoo yet invented. To them, Friday is just another day, and thirteen is just another number. There probably is not a luck charm in a boatload of submariners.

The Submariner's Insigne

Our Older Subs Are Often Used for Laying Mines

CHAPTER XIII

The Submarine in Action Today

THE primary purpose of the submarine, or "mission," as it is designated in Navy language, was and still is to destroy enemy capital ships. For this purpose it employs its main weapon, which is the most powerful and devastating projectile ever invented—the torpedo. Properly placed, a torpedo could send the Empire State Building in New York crumbling into ruins. But the cost of a torpedo ranges up to $10,000, and because of its bulk the supply that can be carried on a submarine is limited. When its stock of torpedoes is exhausted, the submarine must return to its base or to a supply ship for more. That is why the submarine rises to the surface and uses its three-inch or four-inch deck gun (sometimes it is a five-inch or six-inch gun) for the destruction of minor vessels and the run-of-the-mill merchant ships. Shells cost but little, and a generous supply can be carried aboard. To waste a torpedo upon such small fry as trawlers or tugs, for example, would be like using a club, instead of a fly-swatter, to kill a fly.

TWELVE THOUSAND MILES—PLUS

The American submarines of the first World War vintage, which includes the O-boats, the R-boats, and the S-boats which are still in service, are of limited cruising radius; consequently, they are employed mainly for coastal defense, scouting, patrol work, mine laying, and training purposes. Uncle Sam's undersea leviathans of today are known as "fleet" or "cruiser" submarines. These are speedy enough to accompany battle squadrons far from our shores and are capable of covering many thousands of miles without returning to a base or to a mother ship for refueling. The cruising radius of the modern submarine is officially and modestly admitted to be "12,000 miles, plus." What it actually is depends upon so many variable factors that a categorical reply would be as impossible as the answer to "How much does a heavy stone weigh?" Wind and weather conditions, for example, and the speed of navigation, and the proportion of the time spent on the surface and

50

submerged—these are such factors. The Japanese boast that under good conditions their submarines (known as I-boats) have a cruising radius of 26,000 miles, which is equivalent to a trip around the world and then some. Confidentially and off the record, few Yankee submariners would admit that their ships were not capable of doing as much.

A FULL-TIME JOB

With the advent of World War II, the functions of the submarine have been extended. One of its important duties today is to scout for enemy vessels and report their positions; another is to patrol definite areas, perhaps with orders to attack any enemy ship that enters them. A further function is to reconnoiter enemy areas, blockade enemy ports, and lay mine fields. Still another of its important missions is to escort convoys—hiding near the center, and thus being screened, but prepared to dive under the convoyed ships and attack the surface vessels or submarines of the enemy. And last but not least of the submarine's duties is to prey on enemy commerce, hunting either as a lone raider or in "wolf packs," a technique so highly developed by the Germans.

MIDGETS OF THE DEEP

From abroad come reports of a class of small German submarines (all German underwater craft are classed as U-boats) of only 250 tons displacement, specifically designed for coast-defense work and for commerce raiding within limited areas. They bear the symbols U-1 to U-24, and were built about 1936-37. The cruising radius of these vessels is probably limited to about 2,500 miles. They carry crews of around twenty men and are equipped with three torpedo tubes. Italy and Russia are credited with submarines of a somewhat similar type. The advantage of these vessels lies in the fact that they can be produced in quantity and at small cost.

A unique type of submarine, so small that it must be transported on a large vessel and dropped overboard near the scene of action, is the long-whispered-about "two-man torpedo" manned by members of Japan's suicide squad, which made its debut during the attack on Pearl Harbor on December 7, 1941 and later figured in the abortive attack on Sidney, Australia. These miniature craft, which are manned by a crew of two, carry two torpedoes in their bows and a single mine in their sterns. The latter weapon is designed to blow up an enemy ship, if chance offers, by backing up into it—a suicide job, to be sure! These little wasps are only 45 feet long and about 5 feet wide; they have a short periscope and are driven by batteries and electric motors that send them under water at the remarkable speed of about 20 knots. Their cruising range is about 200 miles. And they are small enough to pass through, or even over, the standard submarine nets.

The Japanese "Two-Man Torpedo"

AN OLD STORY RETOLD

The pattern of today's submarine warfare is following to a striking degree that of the first World War. In both cases the initiative was taken by German submarines. In both cases the sinkings of merchant ships early rose to alarming proportions, including, in the present war, extensive destruction of tankers on our Atlantic Coast. In both cases the submarines sank major warships and thereby crashed the newspaper headlines and, in the present war, interrupted radio programs with breathless news flashes. Even the feat of Lieutenant Weddigen was duplicated by Lieutenant Prien, who miraculously penetrated the tortuous channels, mine fields, and nets laid in Scapa Flow, evaded the British destroyers, and torpedoed the British "floating fortress" of 29,150 tons, the *Royal Oak*, on October 14, 1939. This feat was followed in due course by the torpedoing of other great ships, including the carrier *Illustrious* on July 3, 1940, the carrier *Ark Royal* on November 13, 1941, and the battleship *Barham*, on November 25, 1941. The first American warship to fall victim to the U-boat was the destroyer *Reuben James*, sunk west of Iceland while on convoy duty October 31, 1941—five weeks before we had entered the war officially. American submarines, according to news dispatches supplemented only by brief communiqués of a general nature, have sunk Japanese ships in the China Sea and in Japanese home waters. An enemy aircraft carrier, transports, and other vessels sunk in the Strait of Macassar were victims of American undersea boats. During 1942, many American submarine captains were decorated with the Navy Cross, an honor that is not awarded for mere routine performances. Both British and Italian submarines have been reported as active in the Mediterranean Sea.

PIG BOATS OF TODAY AND TOMORROW

That the modern submarine is an infinitely more effective weapon against its foes as well as a safer vessel for its crew than was its predecessor of twenty-five years ago cannot be doubted; that the methods of defense against it have kept pace can be and is being doubted. Because it has a far greater cruising radius, it can now maintain its position with the battle fleet. Were the Battle of Jutland (in which none of the old, slow-moving submarines participated, because they were un-

able to gain positions) fought today, the role played by the undersea fighters might well make the results of that debatable conflict conclusive. When the modest flotilla of the United Nations came to grips with the superior Japanese naval force in the Straits of Java in March 1942, it was reported to have been stopped by a "wall of Japanese cruiser submarines." And American submarines have been reported as carrying the attack to the very shores of Nippon. Twenty-five years ago the voyages of a small number of United States undersea craft to such comparatively near-by points as Ireland and the Azores were regarded as daring accomplishments—and they were. Today the submarine can submerge more quickly and remain under water for longer intervals; its chances of being caught on the surface are far less than in the first World War. It moves faster and is a greater menace to slow-moving convoys. The improved periscope of today can be raised and lowered in a matter of seconds, in contrast to the laborious technique in use a few years ago; therefore the presence of a submarine is less likely to be detected. Torpedoes today are more dependable, move faster, and are launched in clusters instead of singly, so that they represent vastly increased fire power. Listening devices have been greatly improved.

Perhaps, behind the curtain of censorship, new ways are being devised for catching the undersea fighting vessel. But unless and until a new and more effective salt can be found to put upon the tails of the modern submarines, they will continue to increase their depredations and will continue to share with the modern airplanes their steadily mounting claims to being major factors, perhaps determining factors, in naval warfare.

U. S. Submarines in Surface Formation

CHAS. ROSNEZ.

This remarkable photograph, the first of its kind, was taken through the periscope of an American submarine.   The sinking ship is a Japanese destroyer.

YOUR PURCHASE OF MORE WAR SAVINGS STAMPS AND BONDS WILL MAKE MORE PICTURES LIKE THIS POSSIBLE!

Coachwhip Publications
CoachwhipBooks.com

TANKS

AND HOW TO DRAW THEM

TERENCE T. CUNEO

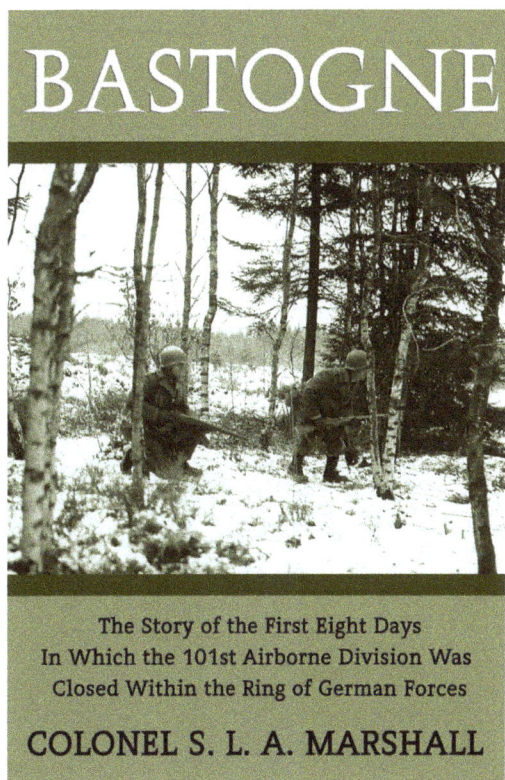

GUNNER
and the DUMBO

Story by Lt. DWIGHT W. FOLLETT, U.S.N.R.
Pictures by DON NELSON

HOW TO DRAW 'PLANES
FRANK A. A. WOOTTON

BASTOGNE

The Story of the First Eight Days
In Which the 101st Airborne Division Was
Closed Within the Ring of German Forces

COLONEL S. L. A. MARSHALL

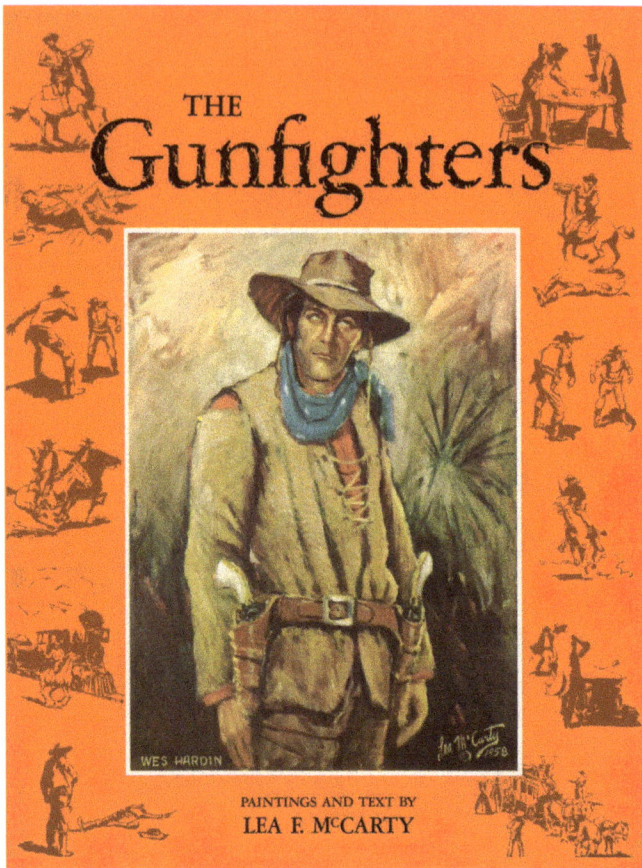

THE
Gunfighters

PAINTINGS AND TEXT BY
LEA F. McCARTY

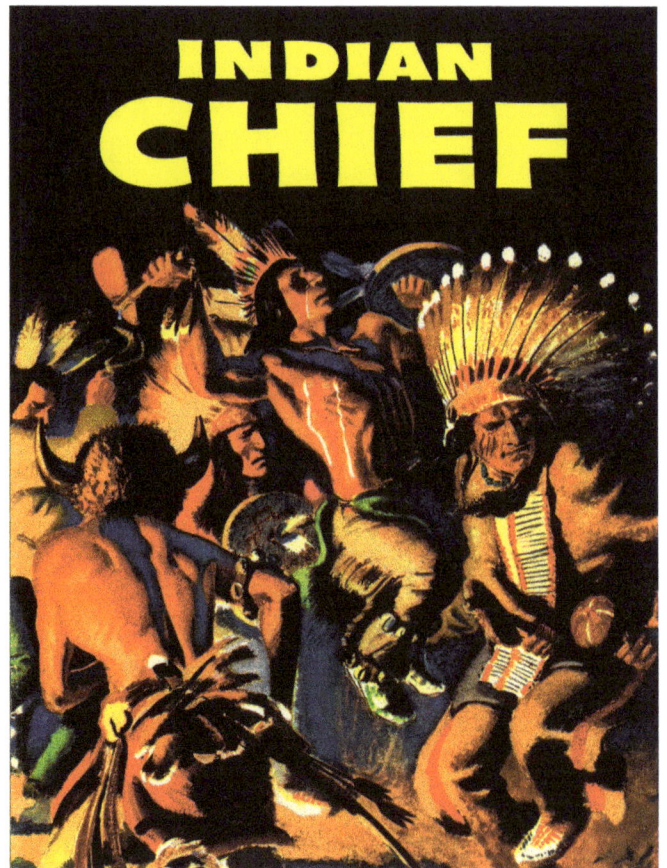

INDIAN
CHIEF

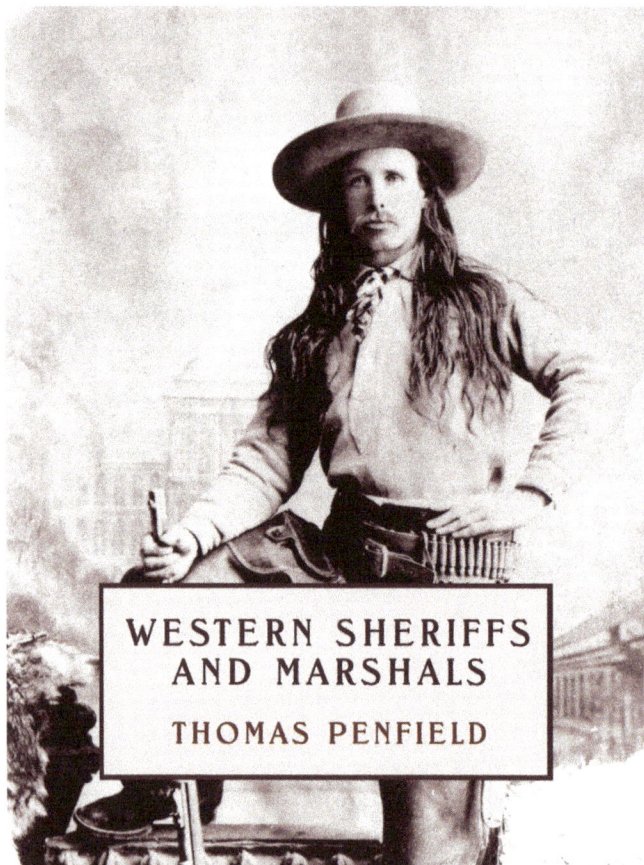

WESTERN SHERIFFS
AND MARSHALS

THOMAS PENFIELD

LARAMIE

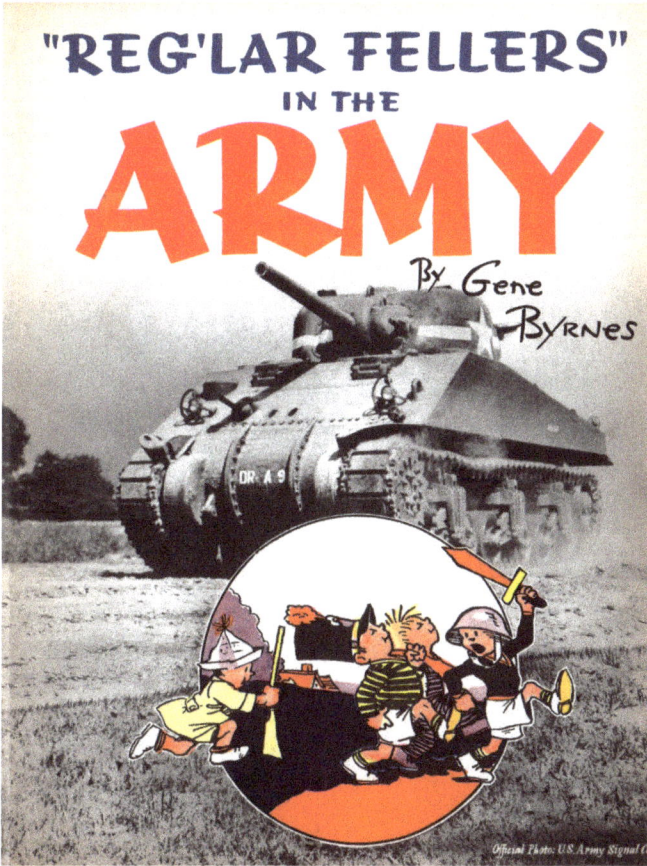

"REG'LAR FELLERS" IN THE ARMY
By Gene Byrnes

Official Photo: U.S. Army Signal C...

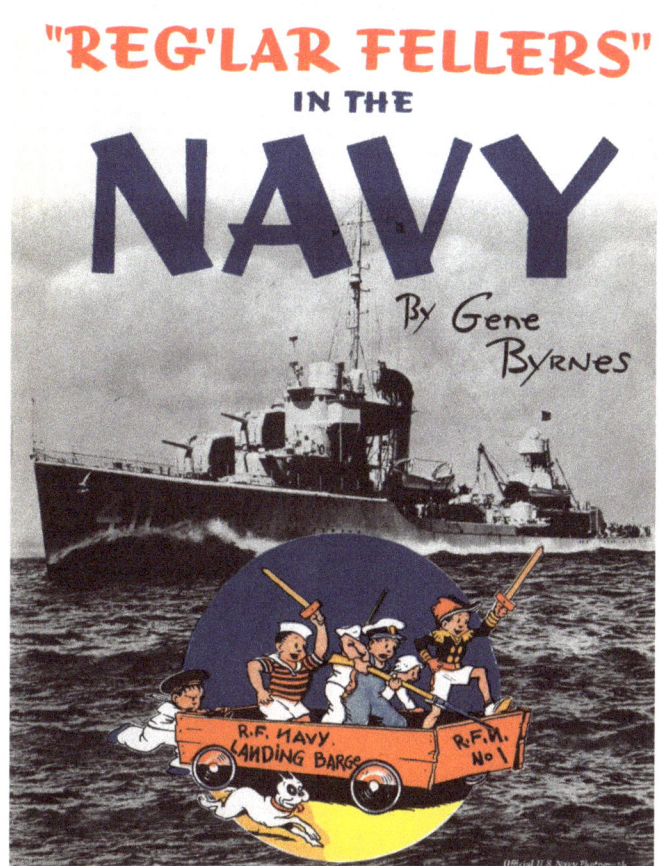

"REG'LAR FELLERS" IN THE NAVY
By Gene Byrnes

R.F. NAVY LANDING BARGE

R.F.N. No 1

Official U.S. Navy Photograph

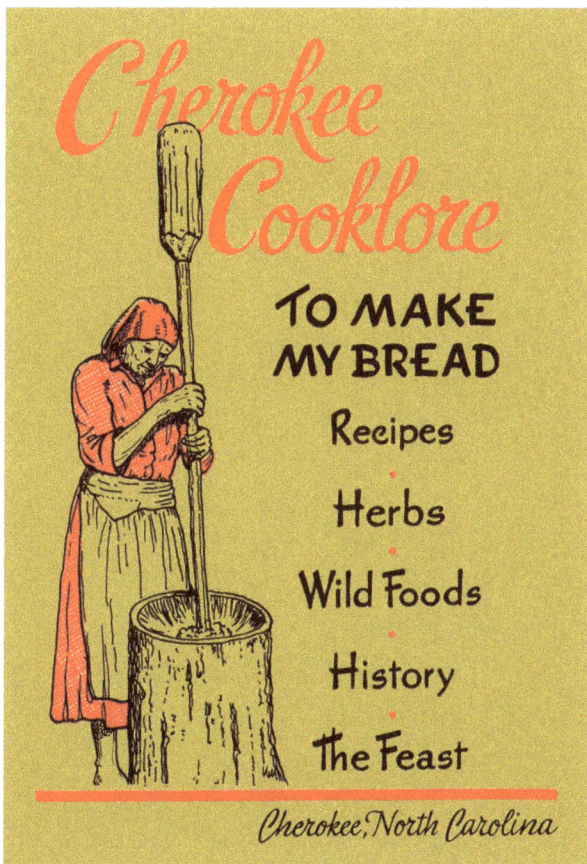

Cherokee Cooklore

TO MAKE MY BREAD

Recipes
•
Herbs
•
Wild Foods
•
History
•
The Feast

Cherokee, North Carolina

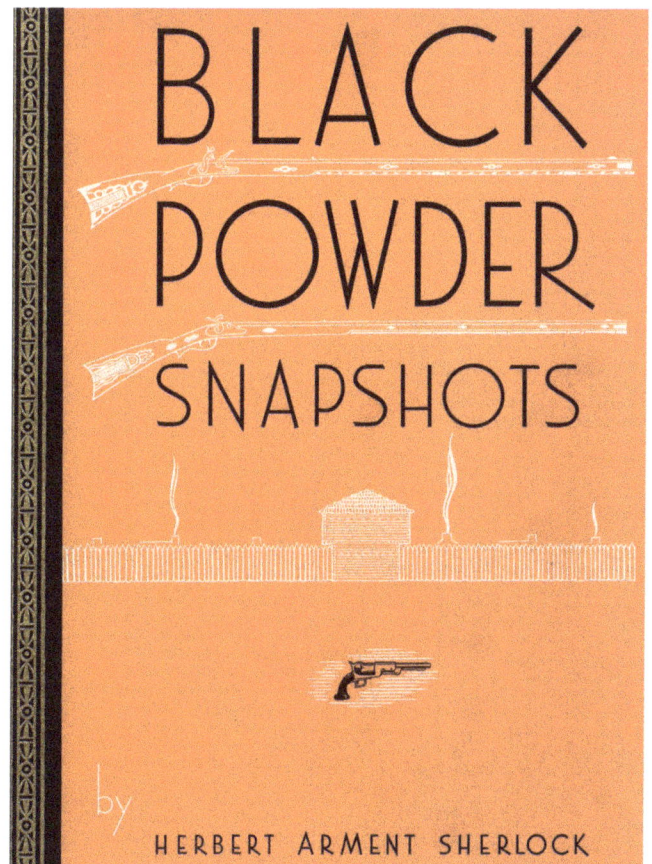

BLACK POWDER SNAPSHOTS

by

HERBERT ARMENT SHERLOCK

www.ingramcontent.com/pod-product-compliance
Lightning Source LLC
LaVergne TN
LVHW070836080426

835509LV00027B/3486